"What could be more ordinary and yet more of an avenue to 'practicing the presence of God' than table grace? Thanks to this original compilation of texts and prayers, we not only make the blessing an intentional act of faith; we also gain access to the treasury of formation wisdom that spans the ages and yet settles around our dinner table."

Susan Muto
Author and Executive Director of the Epiphany Association

✛ ✛ ✛ ✛ ✛

"So often today, the taking of a meal is a barely conscious act — swift, solitary, and unsanctified. What a beautiful alternative opens out in *Table Blessings* — of meals celebrated and sanctified, eaten in the warmth of 'table fellowship' that extends back through time and out around us as well.

"Surely it is a central purpose of the religious life, secular or monastic, that the most ordinary act should become fully conscious and deliberate, that it be understood in the full web of meanings. This beautiful cycle of table blessings seems to me a lovely way to accomplish that."

Carol Lee Flinders
Author of *Enduring Grace* and coauthor of *Laurel's Kitchen*

✛ ✛ ✛ ✛ ✛

"The prayers and readings in *Table Blessings* breathe a spirit of grace, love, and peace that will truly bless each household that brings this beautiful book to the dinner table."

Elise Boulding
International scholar and Quaker peace-activist

✛ ✛ ✛ ✛ ✛

"This most timely book will bring about a humble realization of God's goodness in his gifts, not only of food and drink, but also in the uniqueness of each family member or friend who gathers to break bread. Such a practice centers a Christian household in an intimate communion with the angels and saints, and provides a cosmic reminder of our oneness with the seasons of nature and our unity with all of God's creatures."

George A. Maloney, S.J.
Author and spiritual director

TABLE BLESSINGS

Mealtime Prayers
Throughout the Year

Brother
Victor-Antoine d'Avila-Latourrette
The author of "From a Monastery Kitchen"

AVE MARIA PRESS   Notre Dame, Indiana 46556

© 1994 by Ave Maria Press, Inc., Notre Dame, IN, 46556

International Standard Book Number: 0-87793-538-6

Library of Congress Catalog Card Number: 94-71884

Cover and text design by Elizabeth J. French

Printed and bound in the United States of America.

To the memory of Dom Pierre Minard,
exemplary monk and humble master
of the ways of prayer

CONTENTS

COMMONS / 147

BLESSINGS OF SPECIAL FOODS / 157

PRAYERS OF THANKSGIVING AFTER MEALS / 161

INTRODUCTION

> So, whether you eat or drink, or whatever you do, do everything for the glory of God (1 Cor 10:31, *NRSV*).

Blessings and prayers before and after a meal are part of the earliest Christian tradition, which in turn finds its origin in the ancient Jewish ritual of pronouncing a blessing before the beginning of the meal. Throughout the centuries, Christian communities, Christian families, and individual Christians have always kept the lovely custom of reading a short passage from the Bible followed by a short prayer, usually called "grace," before sitting down to their daily meals. Unfortunately, with the increased secularization of our society, as well as the fast pace of daily life, the first thing we often put aside is the practice of offering thanks to God for his daily gifts to us.

And yet, as history has proven time and again, whenever there is a decline in a certain practice a time of revival usually follows. With the renewal of the liturgy in the last decades, interest has grown in revitalizing the practice of prayer at the table. Many do this in a spontaneous manner, but in the long run, spontaneous prayer at the table can become trivial or difficult to sustain day after day. In some parts of the world (such as Belgium, France, and Italy) the use of prayers and readings following the liturgical cycle is growing in popularity. This practice attunes the believer to the attitudes of the particular season and brings one into spiritual communion with other members of the body of Christ at large. There is a certain wisdom imparted by the Spirit when we participate in the seasons and festivals of the church's year. We are all called to enter into the richness and saving power of the mystery of Christ. We do it concretely by prayer and by listening to the word of God which ultimately forms Christ in each of us.

This collection of readings and prayers for the table is based on the daily and seasonal rhythm of the liturgy. Although mainly inspired by the Catholic tradition, it is meant to be ecumenical in character. The readings are taken from the scriptures, from liturgical texts of the East and the West, and from Christian writings derived from monastic and mystical sources which represent twenty centuries of a continuous and living tradition. The richness of these texts will expose those who use them to the depth and variety of prayer within the Christian tradition. Hopefully, those who pray them together in the context of a shared meal will grow gradually above denominational barriers into that unity which Christ wishes for his church.

Prayer at the table helps to bring communities, families, and friends together. It helps us keep in touch with the Lord at concrete times of the day. It also helps us to remember our brothers and sisters in need. It is not proper for Christians to thank God for his blessings while forgetting the poor or those who are deprived of nourishment. As followers of Jesus, we are called not only to pray for them, but also to share with them from what the Lord has provided for us.

There is something else which is well known but often forgotten—the sacred character of the dinner table. There is a profound link between prayer and the meal itself. All we have to do is recall the many episodes in the gospels when Jesus shares a meal with his disciples and friends. First and foremost is the institution of the eucharist. Among the many other meals the Lord shared with his disciples were the "breaking of bread" at Emmaus on the evening of his resurrection, the wedding feast of Cana, and the multiplication of the loaves and the fishes where the Lord expressed his tender compassion for the hungry crowd and provided food in abundance for them. Again and again the gospel narratives relate the importance that Jesus attributed to food and friendship at the table.

HOW TO USE THIS BOOK

There are many ways in which these readings and prayers can be used on a daily basis. The particular way may change from time to time, according to the specific circumstances. Ideally, one begins with an introduction, which normally should include the sign of the cross. Immediately after, the group or family sits at the table and listens quietly to the reading. The reading sets the tone for the prayer and the meal. It gives us a pause for quiet reflection and creates the particular theme to be developed in the prayer itself. After the reading comes a short responsory. Everyone present should participate by answering the response part. This is followed by the Lord's Prayer which is said together. The Lord's Prayer is probably the most ancient of table prayers which is said to this day by Christians of the East and the West. Then the blessing follows. If one wishes, the person pronouncing the blessing could say it while standing.

In a group situation, someone should be appointed to do the reading, another to recite the verse, and whoever is presiding should pronounce the blessing while everyone else participates by joining in the response and the Lord's Prayer. On a special feast or particular celebration one may begin the prayer with a hymn or refrain sung by all, thus honoring God with joyous song and enriching the experience of all those present at the table. If the group so chooses, they could pray the blessing together, though by nature this prayer is ordinarily said by one person in the name of all. At the end of the blessing, everyone present pronounces the Amen, thus giving their full assent to the prayer.

In an unusual situation (for lack of time or another reason) the reading may be omitted. One would proceed directly to the Lord's Prayer and the blessing. Hopefully, this would be a rare occurrence, for the reading is there to prepare the prayer and to enhance the meal. In some cases, it may create the topic for thoughtful conversation at the table.

These readings and prayers are not meant to be used only for Christian groups or families. They are also meant for the Christian who lives alone and wishes to honor the Lord in a special way at the daily meal. The readings and prayers are meant for both collective and individual use.

The thanksgiving prayer at the end of the meal was purposely written to be short and is simple. It is a basic acknowledgment to God for the gifts received. Again, it can be said collectively or by one person alone.

These readings and prayers should be used following the liturgical calendar and its particular seasons. There are four weeks of ordinary time with enough variety of readings and prayers for the space of a month before they begin to be repeated. For those who wish to honor the saints there is a separate monthly calendar in which their feasts and memorials are kept. We could not provide a special section for each saint, so there are commons in the back which can be applied to the particular saint that a group wishes to commemorate. The saints listed in this collection include those of the first ten centuries which belong to the common heritage of the one undivided church. They are our fathers and mothers in the faith, who through the witness of their lives, contributed to the building up of the body of Christ. Perhaps by honoring them we can work to rediscover our common roots and the unity which Christ wills for his church. Some saints of the last ten centuries are also included here, especially the great mystics such as St. Teresa of Avila, St. Catherine of Genoa, etc., whose writings enlighten the whole Christian church. There are also others such as the humble St. Bernadette, whose gospel way of life is a continual example for us all. In general, the saints presented are recognized by both Catholics and Orthodox, and are honored by many Anglicans, Lutherans, and other Christians. The examples of their lives and their teachings are a source of encouragement and strength on our common journey to God.

Hopefully, the variety found in this collection of prayers will enrich our otherwise ordinary prayer life. They can encourage us to honor the Lord properly and daily for all his benefits to us.

✛ ✛ ✛ ✛ ✛

I wish to acknowledge gratefully some of the persons whose strong support made this work possible. First to Elise Boulding who encouraged me almost twenty years ago to compile the table prayers in use at Our Lady of the Resurrection monastery. This past year she took time to examine these prayers before they were sent to the publisher. Next to Ave Maria Press, in particular to Frank Cunningham and Robert Hamma who showed great interest in the work from the very beginning and gave it their heartfelt support and helpful suggestions. Last, but not least, I wish to express a very special thanks to Anne Poelzl, a dear friend and neighbor. With utmost patience and devotion, she typed the entire manuscript, from page one to the last. This book could not have been produced within the appointed time without her most generous help.

As the psalmist says: "Let us bless the Lord at all times," especially at the table, for providing for our daily nourishment and all our other needs. With St. Paul "let us abound in thanksgiving" for the gifts received.

BR. VICTOR-ANTOINE
February 18, 1994
Feast of St. Bernadette

TABLE PRAYERS FOR ORDINARY TIME

SUNDAY

Reading   Christ, the joy, the truth, and the light of all,
the life of the world and the resurrection.
In his goodness he has appeared to those on earth.
He has become the image of our resurrection,
granting divine forgiveness to all.

Byzantine Kontakion

Responsory

Verse: Make a joyful noise to the Lord, all the earth.
Worship the Lord with gladness;

Response: come into his presence with singing (Ps 100:1-2).

The Lord's Prayer

Blessing   O God, you dispel the darkness of our lives
with the shining glory of the resurrection of your Son.
Bless this food and drink which you provide for us,
that being renewed in body and soul,
we may serve you with holiness of life,
through Christ our Lord.
Amen.

MONDAY

Reading   So do not worry about tomorrow: tomorrow will take care of itself.
Each day has enough trouble of its own (Mt 6:34).

Responsory

Verse: Know that the Lord is God.
It is he that made us, and we are his;

Response: we are his people,
and the sheep of his pasture (Ps 100:3).

The Lord's Prayer

Blessing   We bless you, O Lord,
for your steadfast love
and for your wonderful works among us.
For you satisfy those who are thirsty
and the hungry you fill with good things.
Glory to you, O Lord,
for being the provider of food for our bodies
and the true nourishment of our souls.
Amen.

TUESDAY

Reading   So if in Christ there is anything
that will move you, any incen-
tive in love, any fellowship in
the Spirit, any warmth or
sympathy—I appeal to you,
make my joy complete by
being of a single mind, one in
love, one in heart and one in
mind (Phil 2: 1-2).

Responsory

Verse: Enter his gates with thanksgiving,
and his courts with praise.

Response: Give thanks to him, bless his name (Ps 100:4).

The Lord's Prayer

Blessing   Merciful God,
You are great in compassion
and your tenderness for us is without measure.
We ask you to give us today our daily bread,

and also to provide for the needs
of all your hungry children around the world.
Through Christ your Son and our Lord.
Amen.

WEDNESDAY

Reading   The soul is kissed by God in its innermost regions, where interior yearning, grace, and blessing are bestowed. It is a yearning to take on God's gentle yoke, it is a yearning to give itself to God's way (St. Hildegard of Bingen).

Responsory

Verse: For the Lord is good;
his steadfast love endures forever,

Response: and his faithfulness to all generations (Ps 100:5).

The Lord's Prayer

Blessing   Lord, Jesus Christ,
we ask you to bless
the food and the drink set at this table.
May they become the sign of your life in us,
and may your love make us one.
Amen.

THURSDAY

Reading   Look at the birds in the sky. They do not sow or reap or gather into barns; yet your heavenly Father feeds them. Are you not worth much more than they are? Can any of you, however much you worry, add one single cubit to your span of life? And why worry about clothing? Think of the flowers growing in the fields; they never have to work or spin; yet I assure you that not even Solomon in all his royal robes was clothed like one of these. Now if that is how God clothes the wildflowers growing in the field which are there today and thrown into the furnace tomorrow, will he not much more look after you, you who have so little faith? (Mt 6:26-31).

Responsory

Verse: All your creatures look to you,

Response: to give them their food in due season (Ps 104:27).

The Lord's Prayer

Blessing   O thou who clothes the lilies of the field
           and feeds the birds of the air,
           who leads the sheep to pasture
           and the hart to the water's side,
           who has multiplied loaves and fishes
           and converted water to wine,
           do thou come to our table
           as giver and guest to dine.
           Amen.

                          Old English Table Prayer

FRIDAY

Reading   In love, the gates of my soul spring open, allowing me to breathe a new
           air of freedom and forget my own petty self. In love, my whole being
           streams forth out of the rigid confines of narrowness and self-assertion,
           which makes me a prisoner of my own poverty and emptiness
           (Karl Rahner).

Responsory

Verse: The Lord is merciful and gracious,

Response: slow to anger and abounding in steadfast love (Ps 103:8).

The Lord's Prayer

Blessing   Blessed you be, O God our Father,
           in Jesus, your Son,
           who became human
           and died on the cross
           in order to lead us back to you.
           Grant us the grace to walk in the light of your love.
           Bless this food and drink of your servants,

which we are about to partake
in the name of the same Jesus your Son.
Amen.

SATURDAY

Reading   I have loved you
just as the Father has loved me.
Remain in my love.
If you keep my commandments
you will remain in my love,
just as I have kept my Father's commandments
and remain in his love.
I have told you this
so that my own joy may be in you
and your joy be complete.
This is my commandment:
love one another,
as I have loved you (Jn 15:9-12).

Responsory

Verse: I find my delight in your commandments,
because I love them.

Response: I revere your commandments, which I love,
and I will meditate on your statutes (Ps 119:47-48).

The Lord's Prayer

Blessing   Father of mercies,
in you is the source of life
and in your light we see light.
Strengthen us with the nourishment of this meal,
and may Christ, your Son,
dwell in our hearts in love,
both now and forever.
Amen.

SECOND WEEK

SUNDAY

Reading   In truth, this day is called holy,
for it is the first day among the sabbaths,
the day of the king and Lord.
It is the feast of feasts, the season of seasons,
in which we bless Christ for evermore.
Come, O faithful, on this glorious day
in which we commemorate the resurrection
to participate in the kingdom of Christ,
and let us drink the new fruit of the vine
which is given for our rejoicing.
Let us praise the Lord for he is God forever more!

Byzantine Matins

Responsory

Verse: This is the Lord's doing;
it is marvelous in our eyes.

Response: This is the day that the Lord has made;
let us rejoice and be glad in it (Ps 118:23-24).

The Lord's Prayer

Blessing   We bless you, Lord our God,
            for through the blood of your Son
            you have reconciled us with you
            and through his glorious resurrection
            you have granted joy to the world.
            Bless our bread, fruit of the earth
            and bless our drink,
            that both may renew us in mind and body
            as we journey toward
            the eternal feast in your kingdom,
            through Christ our Lord.
            Amen.

MONDAY

Reading   "I am the first to accept loneliness as far as it is livable; but I am also the
            first to rejoice in the communion of saints on earth. And this consists in
            love which respects the suffering of the other, and sees the glory in it,
            and does not try to fight it or take it away, because it would mean taking
            the ultimate glory away. To see one's own suffering as glory is impos-
            sible, but it is very easy to see the other person's suffering as glory; and
            this is the transfiguring strength of love" (*Mother Maria, Her Life in
            Letters*).

Responsory

Verse: But know that the Lord has set apart
            the faithful for himself;

Response: the Lord hears when I call to him (Ps 4:3).

The Lord's Prayer

Blessing   O Eternal God, origin of divinity,
            good beyond all that is good,
            fair beyond all that is fair,
            in whom there is calmness, peace, and concord:
            make up for the dissensions
            which divide us from each other.

And bring us back into the unity of love,
that to your divine nature we may bear some resemblance.
Bless the food and drink of your servants,
through the grace, the mercy,
and the tenderness of your only begotten Son,
Jesus the Christ, our Lord.
Amen.

Based on a Prayer by
Dionysius of Alexandria

TUESDAY

Reading   "See my children, the kingdom of God is now within us. The grace of the Holy Spirit shines forth and warms us and is overflowing with many and varied scents into the air around us, regales our senses with heavenly delight, as it fills our hearts with inexpressible joy" (St. Seraphim of Sarov).

Responsory

Verse: For you, O Lord, have made me glad by your work;

Response: at the works of your hands I sing for joy (Ps 92:4).

The Lord's Prayer

Blessing   We pray and beseech you,
O good God and the lover of humankind,
to send down to us the Paraclete,
the Spirit of truth, holy, and life-giving.
He spoke in the law of old
and by the holy prophets and apostles.
He is everywhere present,
and fills all things with joy.
May your Holy Spirit bless the food
spread upon this table,
that we may be strengthened by it for your service.
And may he lead us all to the eternal banquet of heaven.
We ask this through Christ our Lord.
Amen.

Paraphrased from the Coptic Liturgy

WEDNESDAY

Reading   "Work is the natural exercise and function of both man and woman. …
             Work is not primarily a thing one does to live, but the thing one lives to
             do. It is, or it should be, the full expression of the worker's faculties, the
             thing in which he finds spiritual, mental, and bodily satisfaction, and
             the medium in which he offers himself to God" (Dorothy L. Sayers).

Responsory

Verse: Unless the Lord builds the house,
             those who build it labor in vain.

Response: Unless the Lord guards the city,
             the guard keeps watch in vain (Ps 127:1).

The Lord's Prayer

Blessing   Blessed be you God, our Maker,
             for you taught us by the word and example of Christ,
             that we must toil the land
             and work honorably in this world.
             Grant us our daily nourishment of mind and body,
             and provide also for the daily necessities
             of all your children around the world.
             We ask you this through Christ our Lord.
             Amen.

THURSDAY

Reading   Let the Word of Christ, in all its richness, find a
             home with you. Teach each other and advise each
             other, in all wisdom. With gratitude in your
             hearts sing psalms and hymns and inspired
             songs to God (Col 3:16).

Responsory

Verse: Your word, O Lord, for ever stands
            firm in the heavens:

Response: your truth lasts from age to age,
            like the earth you created.

The Lord's Prayer

Blessing   Lord God, by the power of your Word
            you made heaven and earth and created all things.
            In the fullness of time you sent your Son into the world,
            the Word made flesh, to reconcile us with you,
            and to teach us how to live as brothers and sisters
            in the harmony that belongs to your children.
            Hear us, as we humbly pray to you,
            to give us and to bless our daily bread.
            Teach us, also, that in sharing this bread
            with those that are hungry,
            we come closer to sharing in your divine life,
            which you give us in Christ, your Son and our Lord.
            Amen.

FRIDAY

Reading   "I awoke this morning with the feeling—very strong—I belong to some-
            one to whom I owe devotion. I recalled an early love and that joyous
            sense of being not my own, but of belonging to someone who loved me
            completely. To put love into action, we must do all for the love of God.
            It is out of our common lives, filled with ordinary actions, that we are
            supposed to increase in love, to become saints" (Dorothy Day).

Responsory

Verse: It is good to give thanks to the Lord,
            to sing praises to your name, O Most High;

Response: to declare your steadfast love in the morning,
            and your faithfulness by night (Ps 92:1-2).

The Lord's Prayer

Blessing	We bless you, O God
	for the word and example of Jesus, the Christ,
	who revealed your love to us
	and instructed us to walk in the ways of love,
	the most cherished of your commandments.
	As we gather at this table to partake of this meal
	we ask you to bless our nourishment
	and to bring us one day
	to love's eternal feast in your kingdom,
	through Christ our Lord.
	Amen.

SATURDAY

Reading	Lift up your heart to God, sometimes even during your meals, and when you are in company; the least little remembrance will always be acceptable to him. You need not cry very loud; he is nearer than we are aware of (Br. Lawrence of the Resurrection).

Responsory

Verse:	Teach me your way, O Lord,
	that I may walk in your truth;
Response:	give me an undivided heart to revere your name (Ps 86:11).

The Lord's Prayer

Blessing	God our Father,
	Creator of all good things,
	you give us as food the fruits of the earth
	rendered fruitful by the work of human hands.
	Bless this meal and those who share it with us,
	and make us always mindful
	of the work and suffering
	of those who labor and toil the land.
	We ask you this through Jesus, your Son and our Savior.
	Amen.

Our Father
in heaven...

THIRD WEEK

SUNDAY

Reading   Christ, the sacrifice that was offered for us, is the father of the world to come. He puts an end to our former life, and through the regenerating waters of baptism in which we imitate his death and resurrection he gives us the beginning of a new life. The knowledge that Christ is the Passover Lamb who was sacrificed for us should make us regard the moment of his immolation as the beginning of our lives (from an ancient Easter homily by Pseudo-Chrysostom).

Responsory

Verse: Christ loved us, and poured out his blood
             to free us from our sins.

Response: To him be glory and dominion forever.

The Lord's Prayer

Blessing   Lord God, source of all life,
you grant joy and peace to the world
through the resurrection of your only begotten Son,
the Lord Jesus Christ.
May he dwell forever in our hearts
and through the partaking of this meal,
may he grant strength and renewal to our mortal bodies.
We ask you this through the same Christ our Lord.
Amen.

MONDAY

Reading   If I lose gentleness, I lose a basic condition for uncovering the presence of God. I already am in the depths of my being. Gentleness is thus a pathway to the life of prayer (Adrian van Kaam).

Responsory

Verse: Learn from me for I am meek
and gentle of heart, says the Lord,

Response: and you will find true rest for your souls.

The Lord's Prayer

Blessing   Generous God, source of all goodness,
you make yourself known to us
through the love of Christ,
our humble and gentle master.
He teaches us to discover you anew
in the events of each day.
Bless, O Lord, we pray,
this food and this drink
which we receive from your bounty,
and may we enjoy forever
the protection of your love.
Amen.

TUESDAY

Reading   "Yahweh says this: Act uprightly and justly; rescue from the hands of the oppressor anyone who has been wronged, do not exploit or ill-treat the stranger, the orphan, the widow; shed no innocent blood in this place" (Jer 22:3).

Responsory

Verse: For the Lord is righteous;
         he loves righteous deeds;

Response: the upright shall behold his face (Ps 11:7).

The Lord's Prayer

Blessing   Lord, our God,
         through the example of your only Son,
         our Lord Jesus Christ,
         you encourage us to walk
         the path of justice and peace
         with special concern and love
         for the poor, the oppressed, the downtrodden.
         As we partake of this meal in your presence,
         teach us to alleviate the hunger and suffering
         of our brothers and sisters around the world,
         through the same Jesus, your Son and our Lord.
         Amen.

WEDNESDAY

Reading   If you wish to draw the Lord to you, approach him as disciples to a master, in all simplicity, openly, honestly, without duplicity or idle curiosity. He is simple and uncompounded and he wants the souls that come to him to be simple and pure. Indeed, you will never see simplicity separated from humility (St. John Climacus).

Responsory

Verse: Good and upright is the Lord.

Response: He leads the humble in what is right (Ps 25:8-9).

The Lord's Prayer

Blessing   Lord Jesus Christ, our God,
           you blessed the five loaves
           and with them you fed thousands:
           do the same, O Lord,
           with this food and drink,
           multiply them in this room
           and throughout the world.
           Sanctify all the faithful
           who shall partake of them,
           and lead us all to the banquet
           of eternal life.
           Amen.

                        Byzantine Blessing, Paraphrased

THURSDAY

Reading   Next to grace, time is the most precious gift of God, yet how much of
           both we waste. We say that time does many things. It teaches us many
           lessons, weans us from many follies, strengthens us in good resolves,
           and heals many wounds. And yet it does none of those things. Time
           does nothing. But time is the condition of all these things which God
           does in time. Time is full of eternity. As we use it so shall we be. Every
           day has its opportunities, every hour its offer of grace (Henry E.
           Manning).

Responsory

Verse: So teach us to count our days

Response: that we may gain a wise heart (Ps 90:12).

The Lord's Prayer

Blessing	Let us bless the Lord for his steadfast love
	and for his wonderful works in our midst,
	for he satisfies those who are thirsty
	and the hungry he fills with good things.
	Glory to you, O Christ the Lord,
	the provider of the food for our bodies
	and the true nourishment of our souls.
	Amen.

FRIDAY

Reading	Divine providence is not in baskets lowered from the sky, but through the hearts and hands of those who love God. The child without food and without shoes made the proper answer to the cruel-minded person who asked: "But if God loved you, wouldn't you have food and shoes?" The younger replied: "God told someone, but they forgot" (George Buttrick).

Responsory

Verse:	Power belongs to God,
	and steadfast love belongs to you, O Lord.
Response:	For you repay to all
	according to their work (Ps 62:11-12).

The Lord's Prayer

Blessing	Lord Jesus Christ,
	you are the true Bread of Life
	that came down from heaven
	to feed all those who are hungry for you.
	As we prepare ourselves to partake of this meal,
	we ask you to bless this food and this drink
	which we receive from your hands.
	As you provide for our needs today,
	help us to provide for the needs of others,
	especially those who have less than we do.
	Amen.

SATURDAY

Reading   When humility delivers us from attachment to our own works and our own reputation, we discover that perfect joy is only possible when we have completely forgotten ourselves. And it is only when we pay no more attention to our own life, and our own reputation, and our own excellence, that we are at least completely free to serve God in perfection for God's own sake alone (Thomas Merton).

Responsory

Verse: Bless the Lord, O my soul,
            and all that is within me, bless his holy name.

Response: Bless the Lord, O my soul,
            and do not forget all his benefits (Ps 103:1-2).

The Lord's Prayer

Blessing   Stretch forth, O Lord,
            your helping hand from heaven,
            and bless the food
            and nourishment of your people.
            May all those who partake of it
            be found worthy to share
            in the banquet of your heavenly kingdom.
            We ask you this through Christ our Lord.
            Amen.

FOURTH WEEK

SUNDAY

Reading Since you have been raised up to be with Christ, you must look for things that are above, where Christ is, sitting at God's right hand. Let your thoughts be on things above, not on the things that are on the earth, because you have died, and now the life you have is hidden with Christ in God. But when Christ is revealed—and he is your life—you, too, will be revealed with him in glory (Col 3:1-4).

Responsory

Verse: But we believe that, if we died with Christ,
then we shall live with him too.

Response: We know that Christ has been raised from the dead
and will never die again. Death has no power over him any more
(Rom 6:8-9).

The Lord's Prayer

Blessing Your resurrection, O Christ our Savior,
has enlightened the whole world,
and given new life to all creation,
previously enslaved to corruption.

Table Prayers for Ordinary Time

With the angels and archangels of heaven
today we sing and proclaim your resurrection.
As we worship you here on earth,
make us worthy to partake of this meal
with pure heart and pure mind,
while we await your coming in glory.
Amen.

MONDAY

Reading   What is a charitable heart? It is the heart of him who burns with pity for all creation. … He looks at the creatures and his eyes are filled with tears. His heart is filled with deep compassion and limitless patience. He overflows with tenderness, and cannot bear to see or hear any evil or the least grief endured by the creature (St. Isaac the Syrian).

Responsory

Verse: The Lord delights in those who revere him,

Response: in those who wait for his love.

The Lord's Prayer

Blessing   O Lord, bless this food,
created by you, that it may be
a means of health to all.
Grant by this invocation of your holy name
that all who partake of it
may receive health of body and soul.
We ask you this through Christ our Lord.
Amen.

Roman Ritual

TUESDAY

Reading   If God allows some people to pile up riches instead of making themselves poor as Jesus did, it is so that they may use what he has entrusted to them as loyal servants, in accordance with the master's will, to do spiritual and temporal good to others (Charles de Foucauld).

Responsory

Verse: It is well with those who deal generously and lend,
who conduct their affairs with justice.

Response: They have distributed freely,
they have given to the poor;
their righteousness endures forever;
their horn is exalted in honor (Ps 112:5, 9).

The Lord's Prayer

Blessing   Father in heaven,
through the words and example of Jesus
you show us your predilection
for the poor and the needy.
Teach us to share with them
what we have received from your abundance.
Bless our food and bless our drink,
that being nourished by them,
we may persevere faithfully in your service.
We ask this through Jesus your Son.
Amen.

WEDNESDAY

Reading   Prayer looks out all the time toward God and stretches toward God with desire. Jeremy Taylor describes it wonderfully when he says: "Prayer is only the body of the soul. Desire are its wings!" (Evelyn Underhill).

Responsory

Verse: Bless the Lord, O my soul.
               O Lord my God, you are very great.

Response: You are clothed with honor and majesty,
               wrapped in light as with a garment (Ps 104:1-2).

The Lord's Prayer

Blessing   Lord God,
               from your dwelling you water the hills;
               earth drinks its fill of your gift.
               You make the grass grow for the cattle
               and bring forth wheat from the earth
               and fruit of the vine to cheer our hearts,
               oil to make our faces shine,
               and bread to strengthen our hearts.
               Bless us, O Lord,
               and bless this food which we partake together.
               Bless also those who prepared it for us,
               and give bread to all those that have none.
               Amen.

THURSDAY

Reading   For, as the rain and the snow come down from the sky
               and do not return before having watered the earth,
               fertilizing it and making it germinate
               to provide seed for the sower and food to eat,
               so it is with the word that goes from my mouth:
               it will not return to me unfulfilled
               or before having carried out my good pleasure
               and having achieved what it was sent to do.
                                   Isaiah 55:10-22

Responsory

Verse: The Lord is my portion;
               I promise to keep your words.

Response: I implore your favor with all my heart;
be gracious to me according to your promise
(Ps 119:57-58).

The Lord's Prayer

Blessing   Lord God,
we bless you for giving us your Word,
the Lord Jesus Christ,
as a lamp to guide our steps toward you,
and as clear light for our path.
Bless, we pray, this food and drink
which we receive from your loving hands.
Bless also the food of our neighbors,
and give bread, peace, and joy to the world.
We ask you this in Jesus' name.
Amen.

FRIDAY

Reading   The interior life is like a sea of love in which the soul is plunged and is, as it were, drowned in love. Just as a mother holds her child's face in her hands to cover it with kisses, so does God hold the devout person who seeks him with a sincere heart (St. John Vianney).

Responsory

Verse: As a deer longs for flowing streams,

Response: so my soul longs for you, O God (Ps 42:1).

The Lord's Prayer

Blessing   O Christ, our true God,
bless the food and drink of your servants,
for you are holy always,
now and forever and ever.
Amen.
                              Byzantine Table Prayer

SATURDAY

Reading   Even though human beings differ from one another by virtue of their ethnic peculiarities, they all possess certain common elements and are inclined to meet each other in the world of spiritual values (Pope John XXIII).

Responsory

Verse: May his name endure forever,
          his fame continue as long as the sun.

Response: May all nations be blessed in him;
           may they pronounce him happy (Ps 72:17).

The Lord's Prayer

Blessing   God, our Father,
           teach us to live the gospel
           in a true spirit of joy, simplicity, mercy,
           and love for one another.
           We pray to you to bless the food
           and fellowship shared at this table.
           We ask you this in Jesus' name.
           Amen.

E·P·H·OVRAND·EX·PICIVR·GRÆCO

TABLE PRAYERS FOR THE LITURGICAL SEASONS

ADVENT

FIRST WEEK OF ADVENT

Reading   Besides, you know the time has come; the moment is here for you to stop sleeping and wake up, because by now our salvation is nearer than when we first began to believe. The night is nearly over, daylight is on the way; so let us throw off everything that belongs to the darkness and equip ourselves for the light. Let us live decently, as in the light of day (Rom 13:11-13).

Responsory

Verse: Rejoice, O daughter of Zion,
shout aloud, daughter of Jerusalem.

Response: See, your king is coming to you, Alleluia!
(Roman Office).

The Lord's Prayer

Blessing   O Lord, our God,
help us to prepare for the coming of Christ, your Son.
When he comes, may he find us
eagerly awaiting in joyful prayer.
Send your blessing upon this table
and all those who partake of this meal.
This we ask through Christ our Lord.
Amen.

SECOND WEEK OF ADVENT

Reading   A voice cries, "Prepare in the desert
a way for Yahweh.
Make a straight highway for our God
across the wastelands.
Let every valley be filled in,
every mountain and hill be levelled,
every cliff become a plateau,
every escarpment a plain;
then the glory of Yahweh will be revealed
and all humanity will see it together,
for the mouth of Yahweh has spoken."

Isaiah 40:3-5

Responsory

Verse: A voice cries out in the desert,

Response: prepare a way for the Lord.

The Lord's Prayer

Blessing   Blessed be you, God of our fathers and mothers,
for you have sent John the Baptist
to prepare the way for Christ.
Open our hearts to the joy of Christ's coming,
and may we imitate in our lives
the simplicity and frugality of John the Baptist,
as we await the blessed hope and coming of our Savior,
our Lord Jesus Christ.
Amen.

THIRD WEEK OF ADVENT

Reading Always be joyful, then, in the Lord; I repeat, be joyful. Let your good sense be obvious to everybody. The Lord is near. Never worry about anything; but tell God all your desires of every kind in prayer and petition shot through with gratitude, and the peace of God which is beyond our understanding will guard your hearts and your thoughts in Christ Jesus (Phil 4:4-7).

Responsory

Verse: Drop down dew, O heavens, from above,
     and let the clouds rain down the just one.

Response: Let the earth be opened,
     and bud forth the Savior (Monastic Office).

The Lord's Prayer

Blessing Lord Jesus Christ,
     Son of David
     and radiant star of morning,
     come and dispel the darkness of our night.
     As the church in ancient time
     once cried for you, we cry again with one voice:
     Come Lord Jesus, come!
     Look with mercy upon us
     who await your coming.
     Give us our daily bread,
     and grant us the grace to share one day
     in the eternal banquet of your kingdom.
     Amen.

FOURTH WEEK OF ADVENT

Reading   Behold, the time of our salvation is
at hand.
Prepare yourself, O cavern,
for the Virgin approaches to give
birth to her Son.
Be glad and rejoice, O Bethlehem,
land of Judah,
for from you our Lord shines forth
as the dawn.
Give ear, you mountains and hills
and all lands surrounding Judea,
for Christ is coming to save the
people
whom he had created and whom
he loves.
Byzantine Office

Responsory

Verse: Sound the trumpet in Zion:
for the day of the Lord is near.

Response: Behold, he will come to save us,
Alleluia! (Roman Office).

The Lord's Prayer

Blessing   Blessed be you, Lord Jesus Christ,
you see how troubled we are
by our evil tendencies
and the need we have of your saving help.
You come to visit us
to heal all our wounds.
Grant your blessings upon this
food prepared for our nourishment,
and may we find consolation
in your forthcoming visitation.
Amen.

CHRISTMAS SEASON

December 24: CHRISTMAS EVE

Reading   Let us celebrate, O people,
the prefeast of Christ's Nativity.
Let us raise our minds on high,
going up in spirit to Bethlehem.
With the eyes of our souls let us behold the Virgin
as she hastens to the cave
to give birth to the Lord and God of all.
Prepare, O Bethlehem,
for Eden has been opened to all.
Adorn yourself, O Ephrata,
for the Tree of Life blossoms forth
from the Virgin in the cave.
Her womb is a spiritual paradise planted
with the fruit divine;

if we eat of it, we shall live forever
and not die like Adam.
Christ is coming to restore us
to the image which he made in the beginning.

Byzantine Office

Responsory

Verse: Today you will know the Lord is coming,

Response: and in the morning you will see his glory
            (Roman Office).

The Lord's Prayer

Blessing   Come, Lord Jesus,
            do not delay,
            give new courage to your people
            who trust in your love.
            As we prepare to receive you,
            we ask you to bless this table
            and the food we share.
            Provide for the needs of others,
            until that day in which we shall all feast
            in the eternal banquet of your kingdom.
            Amen.

December 25: CHRISTMAS DAY

Reading   Today Christ is born.
            Today the Savior has appeared.
            Today the angels sing on earth,
            and the archangels rejoice.
            Today the just exult, saying:
            Glory to God in the highest. Alleluia (Roman Office).

Responsory

Verse: Unto us a child is born, Alleluia.

Response: A Son is given to us, Alleluia.

The Lord's Prayer

Blessing   God our Father, we bless you.
You have so loved the world
that you have sent to us your Son,
Jesus, the Word made flesh.
God our Father, we thank you
for this festive meal which brings all of us together
in joy on this day
when we celebrate the birth of your Son.
God our Father, we praise you
for giving us Jesus, God with us,
the light that rises in the night
and dispels all darkness from it.
Amen.

Sunday after Christmas:
FEAST OF THE HOLY FAMILY

Reading   What shall we offer you, O Christ,
who for our sake has appeared
   on the earth as a man?
Every creature which you have
   made offers you thanks:
the angels offer you a song,
the heavens, their star,
the wise men, their gifts,
the shepherds, their wonder,
the earth, its cave,
the wilderness, the manger.
And we offer you a Virgin Mother.
O eternal God, have mercy on us.

Byzantine Office

Responsory

Verse: Our Savior, the dayspring from the east,
has visited us from on high. Alleluia.

Response: And we who were in darkness and shadow
have found the truth,
for the Lord is born of a virgin. Alleluia
(Byzantine Office).

The Lord's Prayer

Blessing Blessed be you, O God,
for through the mystery of the incarnation
of Christ, born into a human family,
you show to the world the beautiful example
of a family united in respect and love.
Teach us the dignity and sanctity of human love,
deepen in us our appreciation of the value of family life,
and help us to live in peace with all people,
that we may be found worthy
to share in your life forever.
We ask this through Christ our Lord.
Amen.

January 1: SOLEMNITY OF MARY, THE MOTHER OF GOD

Reading All of creation rejoices in you, O Mary,
full of grace,
the assembly of angels and the
human race.
O sanctified temple and spiritual
paradise,
the glory of virgins, from whom God
was incarnate
and became a child, our God before
the ages.
He made your body a throne,
and your womb he made more spacious
than the heavens.
All of creation rejoices in you,
Mary, full of grace, glory to you! (St. Basil's Liturgy).

Responsory

Verse: Your blessed and fruitful virginity
is like the bush, flaming yet unadorned,
which Moses saw on Sinai.

Response: Pray for us, O Mother of God.

The Lord's Prayer

Blessing   Eternal God,
as we enter this new year of grace
may we be kept safe
by the unfailing protection of the Mother of God.
Through her you have sent your Son into the world,
who brought us life and salvation to all.
Bless all those present around this table
and the food we are about to partake.
Make us always mindful
of those who have little or no food to eat.
In your loving providence,
provide also for their daily needs.
Through Christ our Lord.
Amen.

Sunday after January 1: EPIPHANY

Reading   From the East came the Magi
to Bethlehem to adore the Lord;
and opening their treasures,
they offered precious gifts:
gold to the great king,
incense to the true God,
and myrrh in symbol of his
      burial. Alleluia.
                    Ancient Antiphon

Responsory

Verse: Begotten of the Father before the daystar shone
or time began, Alleluia,

Verse: the Lord our Savior has appeared on earth today,
Alleluia.

The Lord's Prayer

Blessing   Mighty and ever-living God,
you made manifest the mystery
of your Word made flesh
with the witness of a blazing star.
At seeing it, the Magi worshipped your majesty
and offered you gifts.
Grant that the star of your holiness
may shine forever within our hearts,
and that we may find our treasure
in offering you our humble praise.
Amen.

Mozarabic Liturgy

Sunday after the Epiphany: BAPTISM OF THE LORD

Reading   Let us pass, O faithful,
from Bethlehem to Jordan.
For behold, the light which came
into the darkness
there begins to overcome the night.
Seeing you, O Christ our God,
drawing near to him in the river
Jordan,
John said: "Why are you who are
without defilement
come to your servant, O Lord?
In whose name shall I baptize you?
Of the Father? But you bear him in
yourself.

Of the Son? But you are yourself the Son made flesh.
Of the Spirit? But you know that from your own lips.
You give him to the faithful."
O God who has manifested yourself to the world,
have mercy on us.

Byzantine Liturgy

Responsory

Verse: Today in the Jordan as the Lord was baptized,
              the heavens opened
              and the voice of the Father was heard.

Response: "This is my beloved Son
              in whom I am well pleased" (Byzantine Liturgy).

The Lord's Prayer

Blessing   Almighty, eternal God,
              when the Spirit descended upon Jesus
              at his baptism in the Jordan,
              you revealed him as your own beloved Son.
              Keep us, your children born of water and the Spirit,
              faithful to our calling.
              Strengthen us with the nourishment of this meal
              which has been prepared for us,
              and keep us always safe
              under your loving protection.
              We ask this through Jesus your Son.
              Amen.

LENT

ASH WEDNESDAY

Reading   The lenten spring has come, the light of repentance is being offered to us. Let us enter the season of Lent with joy, giving ourselves to spiritual strife, cleansing our soul and body, controlling our passions as we limit our food, and striving to live by the virtues inspired by the Spirit. Let us persevere in our longing for God so as to be worthy upon the completion of the forty days to behold the most solemn passion of Christ, and to feast with spiritual joy in the most holy Passover of the Lord (Lenten Byzantine Text).

Responsory

Verse: This is the acceptable time,
            the time of penance has come,

Response: the time to atone for our sins
            and to seek our salvation (Roman Liturgy).

The Lord's Prayer

Blessing   Lord, our God, we welcome with joy
the arrival of the lenten season.
Help us in our battle against evil,
and allow us to follow the observance of Lent
with humble and contrite hearts.
Bless our daily nourishment,
and inspire us to share our food
with the poor and the hungry.
We ask you this through Christ our Lord.
Amen.

FIRST WEEK OF LENT (and the days after Ash Wednesday)

Reading   Lent is a journey, a pilgrimage! Yet, as we begin it, as we make the first
step into the "bright sadness" of Lent, we see far, far away our destina-
tion. It is the joy of Easter, it is the entrance into the glory of the
kingdom. And it is this vision, the foretaste of Easter, that makes Lent's
sadness bright and our lenten effort a "Spiritual Spring." The night may
be dark and long, but all along the way a mysterious and radiant dawn
seems to shine on the horizon. "Do not deprive us of our expectation, O
Lover of [humankind]!" (Alexander Schmemann, *Great Lent*).

Responsory

Verse: Armed with God's justice and power,

Response: let us prove ourselves through patient endurance.

The Lord's Prayer

Blessing   God of love and tenderness,
           accept the humble prayers and penance we offer you
           as we undertake the yearly discipline of Lent.
           May our fasting and prayer
           increase in us a hunger for a deeper sharing
           in Christ's death and resurrection.
           Bless the food and drink of your servants,
           that we may be renewed and strengthened
           as we journey toward the joy of Easter.
           Grant this through Christ our Lord.
           Amen.

SECOND WEEK OF LENT

Reading   Let us fast, O faithful, from corrupting
          snares, from harmful passions, so that
          we may receive a new life from the
          Cross of Christ and return with the
          good thief to our initial home. While
          fasting physically, brothers and sisters,
          let us remember also to fast spiritual-
          ly: Let us lose every knot of iniquity,
          and let us tear up all bondage from
          evil. Let us distribute bread to the
          hungry, and welcome into our homes
          those who have no roof over their
          heads, so that upon completing the
          lenten fast we may receive great
          mercy from Christ, our God (Lenten
          Byzantine Text).

Responsory

Verse: Let us turn back to the Lord
and atone for our sins and offenses.

Response: May the Lord show us his mercy
and renew us in heart and spirit.

The Lord's Prayer

Blessing   Almighty and eternal God, in your wisdom and mercy
you have brought us to these holy days of lenten fast.
May they serve us for the purification of our bodies and souls,
and for the controlling of our passions.
Enlightened by our lenten fasting,
we wish to grow inwardly closer to you,
and outwardly closer to our brothers and sisters in need.
Bless this table, our food and those who prepared it for us,
and keep us in good cheer during our pilgrimage
toward the feast of feasts.
Grant this through Christ our Lord.
Amen.

THIRD WEEK OF LENT

Reading   Lent commemorates Israel's forty years
of wandering in the wilderness, those
forty years during which the Chosen
People having left the captivity of
Egypt and crossed the Red Sea, went
forward with faith toward the far-off
promised land, receiving their earthly
food from God in the form of manna
and their spiritual food in the form of
the Ten Commandments. Sometimes
they rebelled and fell into sin, but still
they reached their goal. Lent also
speaks to us of liberation, of
pilgrimage, of crossing an arid desert,

of the divine manna, of a meeting with God on Sinai, and also, of fall and reconciliation (A Monk of the Eastern Church, *The Year of Grace of the Lord*).

Responsory

Verse: Our sacrifice to God is a repentant heart
and a contrite spirit.

Response: A humble and contrite heart, O God,
you will not spurn.

The Lord's Prayer

Blessing We bless you, Almighty God,
and we give thanks to your holy name,
for as you led your Chosen People through the desert,
you fed and sustained them with manna from above.
As we continue our lenten journey,
deign to bless this food and drink at our table,
that being properly renewed in body and spirit,
we may arrive with joy at the feast of your salvation.
We ask this in Jesus' name.
Amen.

FOURTH WEEK OF LENT

Reading Lent recalls the forty days that the Lord Jesus spent in the desert during which he contended with Satan, the tempter. Our Lent must also be a period of fighting against temptation, and especially against the temptation of our most habitual sin. "Thou shalt worship the Lord thy God, and him only shalt thou serve" (Lk 4:8). May it be granted to us, during Lent, to learn and understand these words with which the Lord opposed Satan, and which summarize the whole of the spiritual battle (A Monk of the Eastern church, *The Year of Grace of the Lord*).

Responsory

Verse: You cannot live on bread alone,

Response: but by every word that comes
             from the mouth of God.

The Lord's Prayer

Blessing   Lord Jesus Christ,
             you have shown us that the desert is waiting
             for those who come to it inspired by the Spirit.
             The desert is a place for self-discovery,
             and more than that, a place for meeting God.
             Help us to follow you into the desert land,
             there to fast, pray, and learn anew
             that the false values of self-indulgence and success
             only lead to death and despair,
             and that our only hope lies in the paradox of the cross.
             Bless this food,
             and those who share it together in your name.
             May we all be preserved from evil,
             and led to fullness of life in your kingdom.
             Amen.

FIFTH WEEK OF LENT (and for the days of Holy Week)

Reading   And thus, if Lent is the recovery by the Christian of his faith, it is also
             his recovery of life, of its divine meaning, of its sacred depth. It is by
             abstaining from food that we rediscover its sweetness and learn again
             how to receive it from God with joy and gratitude. It is by "slowing
             down" on music and entertainment, on conversation and superficial
             socializing that we rediscover the ultimate value of human relationship,
             human work, human art, and rediscover all this because very simply
             we rediscover God himself—because we return to him and in him to all
             that which he gave us in his infinite love and mercy (Alexander
             Schmemann, *Great Lent*).

Responsory

Verse: Let us turn away from sin
            and be faithful to the gospel.

Response: For the kingdom of God is at hand.

The Lord's Prayer

Blessing   Lord Jesus,
          you teach us during these lenten days
          to seek God's face
          by the practice of fasting and constant prayer.
          Help us during this blessed time
          to be purified from all sin
          so that we may worthily enter into passiontide
          and sing your praises on Easter day.
          Send your blessing upon this table,
          and upon all those who share it with us.
          May we all be led to the glory of your kingdom.
          Amen.

PASSION SUNDAY

Reading   The Savior has come today to the city
           of Jerusalem,
        to fulfill the scriptures;
        and the children have taken palms into
           their hands
        and spread their garments before him,
        knowing that he is our God,
        to whom the cherubim sing without
           ceasing:
        Hosanna in the highest!
        Blessed are you who show great com-
           passion for our humanity,
        Lord, have mercy upon us.
                       Byzantine Vespers

Responsory

Verse: Rejoice and be glad, O church of God,
for behold, your king comes seated in righteousness.

Response: He comes seated on a foal, and the children sing:
Hosanna in the highest!

The Lord's Prayer

Blessing Blessed are you, Lord our God,
in your only begotten Son, our Lord Jesus Christ.
In his infinite love for humanity
he enters today the city of Jerusalem,
to undergo the sufferings of his passion,
and thus reconcile our lost humanity with you.
Grant us to partake of this meal
in the spirit of the last meals of Jesus with his disciples,
in fellowship and thanksgiving for your tender mercies,
and for all that you have done to save us.
We ask you this in the name of the same Jesus, our Lord.
Amen.

HOLY THURSDAY

Reading   Instructing his friends into the divine mysteries, Jesus, the wisdom of God, prepares a table that gives food to the soul, and mingles for the faithful the cup of the wine of life eternal. Let us all, therefore, draw near the mysterious table, with pure souls let us receive the Bread of Life: Let us remain at the master's side, that we may see how he washes the feet of the disciples and wipes them with a towel, and let us do as we have seen him do, washing one another's feet. For such is the commandment that Christ himself gave to his disciples (Byzantine Matins).

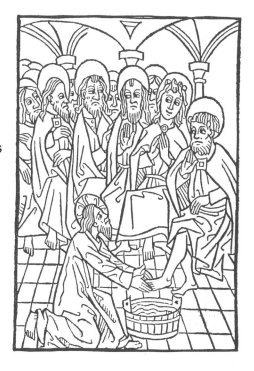

Responsory

Verse: Come, O faithful,
         let us enjoy the master's hospitality,

Response: and partake at the table of immortal life
         in the upper room.

The Lord's Prayer

Blessing   Lord Jesus Christ,
         in your ardent love for your apostles
         you desired to share the Passover meal with them
         on the night before you suffered.
         During the course of that meal,
         you instituted the sacrament of the eucharist
         where you offered to us your own body and blood
         as bread and wine to nourish our souls.

Send your blessings upon this table
and all those who partake of it.
Nourish us with the Bread of Life,
until the day we are called
to the banquet of eternal life.
Amen.

GOOD FRIDAY

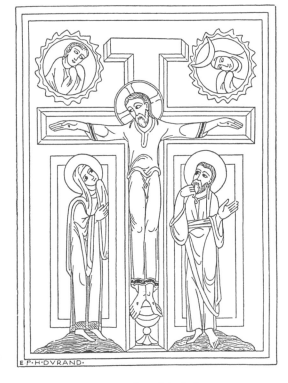

Reading   The whole creation was changed
by fear, when it saw you, O Christ,
hanging on the cross. The sun was
darkened and the foundation of
the earth was shaken for all things
suffered with the creator of all. Of
your own will you have endured
this torment for our sakes. Therefore, we the faithful glorify your
great compassion.

And seeing you hanging on the
cross, O Christ, the Virgin Mother
cried: "O my Son, where is the
beauty of your form? I cannot bear
to look upon you crucified unjust-
ly. Make haste, then, to arise my Son, that I may see on the third day
your resurrection from the dead" (Byzantine Service of the Twelve
Gospels).

Responsory

Verse: You were led as a sheep to the slaughter,
O Christ, our God and King.

Response: As an innocent Lamb, you were nailed
to the cross for our sins.

The Lord's Prayer

Blessing Blessed are you, merciful Father.
You sent to the world your beloved Son,
the Lamb of God, to endure the sufferings of the cross
and thus accomplish the redemption of your people.
Grant that through the mystery of his passion and cross
we may be delivered from darkness and all evil,
and pass from this world to you, Father,
where with Jesus we may glorify you forever.
Bless our nourishment on this day,
that it may give us strength to continue our journey,
toward the glory of Easter.
We ask this in Jesus' name.
Amen.

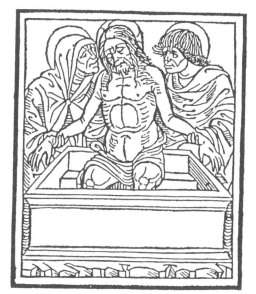

HOLY SATURDAY

Reading   Joseph begged your holy body from
            Pilate, O Lord,
        and anointing it with sweet-smelling
            spices,
        he wrapped it in clean linen and laid it
            in a new tomb.
        The faithful women came to anoint
            you with myrrh,
        weeping bitterly and crying:
        "This is the most blessed sabbath on
            which Christ sleeps,
        but on the third day he shall rise again."
        Therefore, O Lord our God,
        we sing to you a hymn, a song at your burial:
        By your burial you have opened for us the gates of life,
        and by your death you have slain death and hell.
        O God our deliverer, blessed are you!

                                        Byzantine Matins

Responsory

Verse: O happy tomb! You received within yourself
             the creator and the author of life.

Response: O strange wonder! He who dwells on high
             is sealed beneath the earth with his own consent.

The Lord's Prayer

Blessing   Blessed are you, God of the living and the dead,
             today Jesus, your beloved Son, rests in the tomb
             having accomplished the work of our salvation.
             From his tomb new life is being offered to the world,
             and both the living and the dead wait in expectation
             of the glad tidings of the resurrection.
             Bless our food and our drink this day,
             and prepare us through this nourishment
             for the joys of the paschal feast.
             We ask this in Jesus' name.
             Amen.

EASTER SEASON

EASTER SUNDAY

Reading   This is the day of the resurrection, let us be illumined, O Christian people, for this is the day of the sacred pasch of the Lord. Come, and let us drink of the new river, not brought forth from a barren stone, but from the fount of life that springs forth from the sepulchre of Christ the Lord. In the early morning, let us arise, and offer to the master a hymn of praise instead of myrrh, and we shall see Christ, the sun of justice in shining splendor rising from the dead, and giving new life to all (St. John Damascene).

Responsory

Verse: This is the day made by the Lord, Alleluia.

Response: Let us rejoice and be glad in it, Alleluia.

The Lord's Prayer

Blessing   Blessed are you, Lord Jesus,
clothed in the splendor of your resurrection.
You accepted death on the cross for our sake,
and therefore, the power of God raised you on the third day.
Grant us the grace to celebrate this Easter festival
with the new bread of sincerity and truth.
Bless our paschal meal
as you once blessed the meal with your disciples,
and be forever present as guest at our table
until the day we join you in the paschal feast of heaven.
Amen.

SECOND WEEK OF EASTER

Reading   Today a sacred pasch is
revealed to us,
a new and holy pasch.
A mystical pasch, worthy of
veneration,
a pasch, which is Christ, our
redeemer.
A spotless pasch, a great
pasch,
a pasch of the faithful.
A pasch which has opened for us the gates of paradise,
a pasch which sanctifies all the faithful.
With the myrrh-bearing women
let us receive the glad tidings of Christ's resurrection, saying:
"Rejoice and be glad, O Jerusalem,
seeing Christ, your king, like a triumphant bridegroom,
coming forth from the tomb."

St. John Damascene

Responsory

Verse: It is the Lord's Passover,
let us be clothed with gladness, Alleluia.

Response: For Christ has passed from death to life, Alleluia.

The Lord's Prayer

Blessing   Blessed are you, Lord Jesus Christ,
the true Paschal Lamb, and the conqueror over death.
After your resurrection,
you wished to share joyfully with your apostles,
a simple meal of bread and fish.
Bless the food and drink at this table,
and make us partake in the joy your disciples felt
when they discovered your presence in the breaking of the bread.
Amen.

THIRD WEEK OF EASTER

Reading   For all of us Easter is a new
entry into the promised land
of grace. Our Easter joy and
jubilation, our Easter alleluia
has ultimately but one meaning and purpose. We have
been brought into the land of
grace, overflowing with the
milk of God's word, the
honey of the eucharist; into
the land of grace where God
is our Father, Christ our
brother and bridegroom, the
Holy Spirit the quest and comforter of our souls; a land where love is
empress and queen (Pius Parch, *Seasons of Grace*).

Responsory

Verse: This is the chosen and holy day,
first of sabbaths, the feast of feasts,

Response: on which we partake of the new fruit
of the vine and bless Christ forever.

The Lord's Prayer

Blessing   Praise and glory be given to you, God our Father,
            who gives us the joy to partake
            in the rising of Christ to new life.
            May the joy of our paschal celebration
            remain with us all the days of our lives,
            and be forever a sign of your loving presence among us.
            Bless our daily nourishment
            and all those present at this table,
            and make us always mindful of the needs of others.
            We ask you through Christ our risen Lord.
            Amen.

FOURTH WEEK OF EASTER

Reading   Our Lord's sheep will finally
           reach their grazing ground
           where all who follow him in
           simplicity of heart will feed on
           the green pastures of eternity.

           Beloved, let us set out for these
           pastures where we shall keep
           joyful festival with so many of
           our fellow citizens. May the
           thought of their happiness urge
           us on! Let us stir up our hearts,
           rekindle our faith, and long
           eagerly for what heaven has in store for us. To love thus is to be already
           on our way (St. Gregory the Great).

Responsory

Verse: Today all things are filled with light and joy,
            Alleluia.

Response: Heaven and earth celebrate
            the resurrection of Christ, Alleluia.

The Lord's Prayer

Blessing   Lord Jesus Christ,
on the evening of your resurrection,
with eyes of faith and love,
your disciples recognized your presence
during the breaking of bread.
Increase the gift of faith in all of us.
May it daily transform our lives,
and allow us to discover you anew
in our brothers and sisters in need.
Bless this meal and those who partake of it,
and keep us always safe
under the protection of your love.
Amen.

FIFTH WEEK OF EASTER

Reading   Easter week, in Greek, has a very
beautiful name: The Week of Renewal,
which in fact suits the whole of the
paschal time. Jesus wished to die and
to rise again at the threshold of spring.
In the same way that Christmas coincides with the victory of sunlight over
darkness, when the days begin to
lengthen, so Easter coincides with the
renewal of nature, when greenery and
flowers appear.

The universe itself is a symbol of spiritual realities. Springtime speaks
to us, if we know how to interpret God's creation, of inner renewal.
There is a springtime of the soul. Easter, like springtime in nature,
brings us a message of hope. The resurrection of Jesus tells us that we
can be changed (A Monk of the Eastern Church, *The Year of Grace of the
Lord*).

Responsory

Verse: Christ has become our paschal sacrifice, Alleluia.

Response: Let us celebrate the feast with the unleavened bread
           of sincerity and truth, Alleluia.

The Lord's Prayer

Blessing   Blessed are you, God of our fathers and mothers,
           who makes us recall during this blessed season
           the rising of Christ to new life,
           the springtime of our redemption.
           By the power of his resurrection
           grant us true renewal of mind and body,
           that we may walk in the steps of the gospel
           with renewed courage and strength.
           We thank you for this meal,
           which comes to us from your hands.
           May your blessing be upon it,
           and upon all those who share it with us.
           We ask this in Jesus' name.
           Amen.

SIXTH WEEK OF EASTER

Reading   It is the business of the church to preach Christ born among men which
           is Christmas, Christ crucified which is Good Friday, and Christ risen
           which is Easter. And after Easter, 'til November and All Saints, and 'til
           Annunciation, the year belongs to the risen Lord: that is all the full

flowering summer and the autumn of wheat and fruit. All belong to Christ risen.

The resurrection is to life, not to death. Can I not then walk this earth in gladness being risen from sorrow? Is the flesh that was crucified become as poison to the crowds in the street, or is it a strong blossoming out of the earth's humus? (D. H. Lawrence).

Responsory

Verse: Since we have been raised
           to new life with Christ, Alleluia,

Response: let us seek the things
           that are above, Alleluia.

The Lord's Prayer

Blessing   Eternal and merciful God,
           the yearly celebration of the paschal mystery
           renews our covenant of reconciliation with you.
           May this new rebirth we celebrate,
           through the power of the resurrection of Jesus,
           show its effects in the way we act and live.
           Bless the food and drink at this table,
           and make us always mindful
           of the needs of the poor and hungry.
           We ask this through Christ our risen Lord.
           Amen.

THE ASCENSION OF THE LORD

Reading   O Christ, splendor and glory of the Father,
          when we behold your ascension on the holy
              mountain,
          we sing a hymn to the beauty of your
              countenance:
          we bow down to your passion, and venerate
              your resurrection,
          and glorify your noble ascension into heaven.

O Lord, life-giving Christ,
when the apostles saw you ascending upon the clouds,
a great sadness filled them.
They shed burning tears and exclaimed:
"O master, do not leave us orphans,
we are your servants whom you loved so tenderly.
Since you are most merciful,
send down to us your all-holy Spirit
as you have promised to us,
to console us and to enlighten our souls."

Byzantine Vespers

Responsory

Verse: O Lord, the cherubim were amazed at your ascension.

Response: They were dazzled as they beheld
you rising upon the clouds.

The Lord's Prayer

Blessing   O Lord, life-giving Christ,
after fulfilling for us your plan of redemption,
from the Mount of Olives you ascended in glory,
in the presence of your disciples.
You are now enthroned at the right hand of God,
and from there you sent to us the Holy Spirit,
to enlighten, strengthen, and save our souls.
Send your blessing upon us and upon this table today,
as you sent it upon your disciples before your departure,
and may this food strengthen us for your service.
Amen.

SEVENTH WEEK OF EASTER

Reading Throughout the whole period between the resurrection and the ascension, God's providence was at work to instill this one lesson into the hearts of the disciples, to set this one truth before their eyes, that our Lord Jesus Christ, who was truly born, truly suffered, and truly died, should be recognized as truly risen from the dead. The blessed apostles together with all the others had been intimidated by the catastrophe of the cross, and their faith in the resurrection had been uncertain, but now they were so strengthened by the evident truth that when their Lord ascended into heaven, far from feeling any sadness, they were filled with great joy (St. Leo the Great, an ascension sermon).

Responsory

Verse: Christ ascended amid shouts of joy,
        the Lord amid trumpet blasts, Alleluia.

Response: And he is gloriously enthroned
           at the right hand of God the Father, Alleluia.

The Lord's Prayer

Blessing Lord Jesus, Christ, our true God.
          You gloriously ascended into heaven,
          and gladdened the hearts of your disciples
          with the promise of the Holy Spirit.
          Send upon us also, your life-giving Spirit,
          that he may heal us of our infirmities,
          confirm us in the faith, and console us in our affliction.
          Sanctify the food and drink at this table,
          multiply them in this room and throughout the world,
          and bring us all one day to the banquet of eternal life.
          Amen.

PENTECOST

Reading   Behold, we celebrate today the feast
　　　　　　of Pentecost,
the descent of the Holy Spirit,
the fulfillment of the promise and
　　the realization of hope.
How noble and awesome is this
　　great mystery.
Therefore, O Lord and creator of all,
we cry out, "Glory to you."
The Holy Spirit provides every gift.
He inspires prophecy, perfects the
　　priesthood,
grants wisdom to the illiterate,
makes simple fishermen to become
　　wise theologians,
and establishes perfect order in the
　　organization of the church.
Therefore, O Comforter,
equal in nature and majesty with the Father and the Son,
we cry out, "Glory to you."

Byzantine Vespers

Responsory

Verse: Heavenly king, consoler, and Spirit of Truth,
　　　　　　you are present in all places and fill all things.

Response: You are the treasury of blessings
　　　　　　and the giver of life;
　　　　　　come, dwell in us and save our souls, O Holy One!

The Lord's Prayer

Blessing   Come, Spirit of true light. Come, life eternal.
Come, hidden mystery of God. Come, nameless treasure.
Come, that which is beyond words.
Come, person who flees from human comprehension.
Come, source of all courage. Come, true hope of all the saved.

Come, eternal joy. Come, garland unfading.
Come, great God and Lord of our realm.
Come, my life and breath. Come, consolation of my soul.
Come, my joy, my glory, my perpetual delight.
Come, O Spirit of truth,
and bless the food and drink at this table,
and grant that we may be nourished abundantly
with the ineffable gift of your presence.
Amen.

Paraphrased from
St. Simeon the New Theologian

FEASTS OF THE LORD
(during Ordinary Time)

TRINITY SUNDAY

Reading   Thus the Father, the Son, and the Holy Spirit testify that they are in no way disunited in power, even though they are distinguished in persons, because they work together in the unity of the simple and immutable substance. How? The Father creates all things through the Word, who is his Son in the Holy Spirit; the Son is he by whom all things are perfected in the Father and the Holy Spirit; and the Holy Spirit is he by whom all things flourish in the Father and Son, and so these three persons are in the unity of inseparable substance; but they are not indistinct among themselves (Hildegard of Bingen, *Scivias*).

Responsory

Verse: Blessed be the holy creator
and ruler of all things.

Response: The holy and undivided Trinity,
now and forever, and unto ages of ages. Amen.

The Lord's Prayer

Blessing   Almighty God, our help, and our refuge,
the fountain of wisdom and tower of strength.
You know that we can do nothing
without your guidance and help.

Direct us by your divine wisdom and power
so that we may seriously undertake the task
of living our Christian lives
faithfully and diligently according to your will,
that we may be profitable to ourselves and to others
and to the glory of your holy name.
For yours is the kingdom, and the power, and the glory
of the Father, and of the Son, and of the Holy Spirit
now and forever, and unto ages of ages.
Amen.

Antiochian Prayer

THE BODY OF CHRIST AND BLOOD OF CHRIST

Reading   It is indeed a tremendous miracle to see God taking flesh and becoming [human], and a greater miracle still to see him suspended on the cross. But the highest of all miracles, Christ our God, is your ineffable presence under the mystic species. Truly you did institute, through this great sacrament, a remembrance of all your marvels. How merciful of you, O God, to give yourself as food to those who fear you! To recall your covenant forever, and to remember your passion and death until the day of your glorious coming! (Byzantine Text).

Responsory

Verse: The wedding feast of the Lamb has begun, Alleluia!

Response: And his bride is prepared to welcome him, Alleluia.

The Lord's Prayer

Blessing   Lord Jesus Christ, everlasting king,
you are the true high priest,
who offered yourself to the Father upon the cross
in atonement for the sins of the world.
In this selfless act of love and service,
you gave us your incorruptible body for sacred food,
and your most precious blood for life-giving drink.
Make us worthy partakers of these ineffable mysteries,
that one day we may come to share
in the banquet feast of heaven.

Bless the food and drink at this table,
that we may be properly renewed for your service.
Amen.

THE SACRED HEART OF JESUS

Reading   We feel in our souls that the Lord is with us according to his promise: "Behold I am with you always, even unto the end of the world!" The Lord is with us. What more could we desire?

The Lord created us, his children, that we might live and bask in him forever, that we might be with him and in him. And the Lord desires to be with us himself, and in us. The Lord is our joy and our gladness. If the kings and rulers of the nations knew the love of God, they would never make war. War comes to us for our sins, not because of our love. The Lord created us in his love, and bade us live in love and glorify him (Archimandrite Sophrony, *The Writings of Staretz Silouan*).

Responsory

Verse: "Learn from me, for I am meek
and gentle of heart," says the Lord,

Response: "and you will find rest for your souls."

The Lord's Prayer

Blessing   O Lord Jesus Christ, light everlasting;
you shone forth from the Father before the world began.
In your compassion, you opened the eyes of the blind man,
and offered refuge to sinners
in the shelter of your divine heart.
Open the eyes of our hearts
to the mystery of your tender love for us,
and grant us to behold you one day
in the ineffable glory of your kingdom.
Bestow your blessing upon this table
and upon all those dear to us,
and make us always mindful
of the needs of our brothers and sisters.
Amen.

CHRIST THE KING

Reading   Jesus alone is our goal and the fulfillment of our hope. We must attach ourselves to him, who by his divinity is the foundation of our being, and who by his humanity is the bond that unites our being to God. He is the life of our life, the fullness of our capacity. Our first lesson should be a realization of our incomplete and imperfect condition, and our first step should be toward Jesus, who is our ultimate fulfillment. In this search for Jesus, in this adherence to Jesus, is our life, our rest, our strength, and all our power to action.

Never must we act except united with him, directed by him, and drawing life from him (Pierre de Berulle, *On the Life of the Christian in Jesus*).

Responsory

Verse: The reign of the Lord our God Almighty has begun;

Response: let us be glad and joyful and give glory to God.

The Lord's Prayer

Blessing   Lord Jesus Christ, eternal king
and giver of life incorruptible:
look down with your infinite mercy
upon the infirmities and weaknesses of our nature.
Illumine and sanctify us with the light of your divine knowledge.
Shine forth in our darkened hearts,
and make us eager lovers of your kingdom.
Bestow your blessing upon this table,
as you blessed many times
the table of your friends and disciples.
And make us partake one day
in the joy of the heavenly banquet in your kingdom.
Amen.

TABLE PRAYERS FOR SAINTS' DAYS

January 2:
SAINT BASIL THE GREAT AND SAINT GREGORY NAZIANZUS

Reading   The bread you store up belongs to the hungry; the cloak that lies in your chest belongs to the naked; the gold that you have hidden in the ground belongs to the poor. If everyone would take only according to his needs and would leave the surplus to the needy, no one would be rich, no one poor, no one in misery (St. Basil the Great).

Responsory

Verse: Put no confidence in extortion,
          and set no vain hopes on robbery;

Response: if riches increase,
          do not set your heart on them (Ps 62:10).

The Lord's Prayer

Blessing   We bless you, Lord, our God,
           for you enlighten the church of the East and the West,
           with the solid doctrine of our teachers in the faith,
           St. Basil the Great and St. Gregory Nazianzus.
           May we always be ready to live according to these teachings,
           as we seek to follow the path of the gospel
           shown to us by Christ, your Son.
           Bestow your blessing upon our table
           and all those dear to us,
           and make us always mindful of the needs of others.
           We ask you this through Christ our Lord. Amen.

January 4: SAINT ELIZABETH ANN SETON

Reading   So our bodies, as Sisters of Charity, must be neither spared or looked at, no labors or sufferings considered for a moment, but rather only asking,

"What is this for my God!"—seeing everything in that one view, *our God, our eternity.* ...

"This is my commandment, that you love one another as I have loved you." The charity of our blessed Lord in the course of his ministry had these distinct qualities which should be the model of our conduct. It was gentle, benevolent, and universal (St. Elizabeth Ann Seton).

Responsory

Verse: May the mountains yield prosperity for the people,
             and the hills, in righteousness.

Response: May he defend the cause of the poor of the people,
             and give deliverance to the needy (Ps 72:3-4).

The Lord's Prayer

Blessing   Fill our hearts, we beseech you, O Lord,
             with love for you and ardent charity for the poor
             as you did with the heart of Elizabeth Seton.
             We thank you for the dedication of her life
             to the poor and the needy,
             which you set as an example to all Christian people.
             We thank you, also, for the fruits of the earth
             which you provide daily for our nourishment.
             May we always be ready to share them
             with those that have less than we do. Amen.

January 12: SAINT AELRED OF RIELVAUX, ABBOT

Reading   There are four qualities which characterize a friend: loyalty, right inten-
             tion, discretion, and patience. Right intention seeks for nothing other
             than God and natural good. Discretion brings understanding of what is
             done on a friend's behalf, and ability to know when to correct faults.
             Patience enables one to be justly rebuked, or to bear adversity on
             another's behalf. Loyalty guards and protects friendship, in good or bit-
             ter times (St. Aelred, *Spiritual Friendship*).

Responsory

Verse: If love be strong, hot, mighty, and fervent,

Response: there may be no trouble, grief, or sorrow fall
           (St. Thomas More).

The Lord's Prayer

Blessing   Pour into our hearts, O God,
           the Holy Spirit's gift of love,
           that we, clasping each other's hand,
           may share the joy of friendship, human and divine,
           and with your servant Aelred
           draw many to your community of love.
           Through the prayers of St. Aelred,
           bless this food and drink of your servants
           that being nourished by it,
           we may persevere faithfully in your service.
           This we ask through Christ our Lord. Amen.

Adapted from the Anglican Liturgy

January 17: SAINT ANTONY THE GREAT, FATHER OF MONKS

Reading   Through him the Lord cured many of those present who were afflicted with bodily ills, and freed others from impure spirits. He also gave Antony charm in speaking; and so he comforted many in sorrow, and others who were quarreling he made friends. He exhorted all to prefer nothing in the world to the love of Christ. And so monasteries sprang up in the mountains, and the deserts were populated with monks who left their homeland and sought instead citizenship in heaven (St. Athanasius, *Life of St. Antony*).

Responsory

Verse: Holy Father Antony, you equaled Elijah in his zeal,
           and followed John the Baptist in his holy way of life.

Response: You populated the wilderness with monks
           eager to follow in the footsteps of Christ, the Lord.

The Lord's Prayer

Blessing   We praise your name merciful God,
           on this day in which we celebrate
           the memory of Saint Antony.
           Upon hearing the words of the gospel
           St. Antony accepted Christ's invitation
           to leave all things behind in order to follow him,
           and as a true inheritor of the fire of Pentecost
           he led many to fullness of life in the Holy Spirit.
           Therefore we give you thanks, O Lord,
           for the wonders which you accomplished in your saints,
           may their intercession make us ever mindful
           of the good things which we daily receive from you.
           We ask you this through Christ our Lord. Amen.

January 21: SAINT AGNES, VIRGIN AND MARTYR

Reading   The blessed Agnes standing in the midst of the flames with outstretched
           hands, prayed to the Lord: "Almighty God, alone to be adored, to be
           worshipped, to be feared, I bless you, and I glorify your name forever.
           Behold," she said, "that which I desired I already see; that for which I
           hoped, I already hold fast; in heaven I am espoused to him whom on
           earth I loved with all my heart" (Magnificat and Benedictus Antiphons
           of the Roman Office).

Responsory

Verse: Let us keep the feast of Saint Agnes,
           by recalling her faith and suffering.

Response: By the grace of God she overcame death
           and entered into fullness of life.

The Lord's Prayer

Blessing   Almighty Lord, eternal God,
        you alone are the all-merciful one.
        Look down upon us with great mercy today
        as we celebrate with joy,
        the birth of Saint Agnes into eternal life.
        May the power of her example
        daily inspire us to seek your face
        with humble fidelity and trust.
        Bless the food and drink at this table,
        for you are blessed forever and ever. Amen.

January 24: SAINT FRANCIS DE SALES, BISHOP

Reading   If, while the mouth prays, the heart is drawn to the prayer within, then do not resist but let your spirit glide into it silently. Even though the spoken prayer you had resolved to make is not completed, do not trouble yourself. For the devotions of the heart that you have made instead are much more pleasing to God, and more salutary for your soul (St. Francis de Sales).

Responsory

Verse: Happy are those
           [whose] delight is in the law of the Lord,

Response: and on his law they meditate day and night (Ps 1:1-2).

The Lord's Prayer

Blessing   We praise your holy name, O Lord, our God,
        for by the example of St. Francis de Sales
        you remind us that we must
        strive to walk in the ways of the gospel
        by the practice of constant prayer, humility,
        meekness, and service to others.
        Bless the food and drink present here at this table,
        may this nourishment strengthen us for your service.
        Through Christ our Lord. Amen.

January 25:
THE CONVERSION OF SAINT PAUL

Reading   It happened that while he was travelling
to Damascus and approaching the city,
suddenly a light from heaven shone all
round him. He fell to the ground, and then
he heard a voice saying, "Saul, Saul, why
are you persecuting me?" "Who are you,
Lord?" he asked, and the answer came, "I
am Jesus, whom you are persecuting. Get
up and go into the city, and you will be
told what you are to do." The men travelling with Saul stood there speechless, for
though they heard the voice they could see no one. Saul got up from the
ground, but when he opened his eyes he could see nothing at all, and
they had to lead him into Damascus by hand. For three days he was
without his sight and took neither food nor drink (Acts 9:3-9).

Responsory

Verse: You are a chosen instrument, holy apostle Paul.

Response: A vessel of God's grace,
            preacher of truth to the whole world.

The Lord's Prayer

Blessing   O Lord our God,
           through the teaching of your apostle Paul,
           you have made the light of the gospel
           shine throughout the world.
           We thank you for his conversion,
           and we beseech you:
           give us the grace to follow his teaching.
           As we gather around this table
           we ask your blessing on our food
           and on that of all your sons and daughters. Amen.

January 26: SAINTS TIMOTHY AND TITUS

(See Common for the Feasts of Pastors and Confessors, pages 152-153.)

January 28: SAINT THOMAS AQUINAS, PRIEST

(See Common for the Feasts of Pastors and Confessors, pages 152-153.)

FEBRUARY

February 2: PRESENTATION OF THE LORD

Reading

Adorn your bridal chamber, O Zion,
and welcome Christ the King.
Salute Mary, the heavenly gate.
For she, the mother who has never known wedlock,
has brought into the temple
him who shone forth before the ages from the Father,
and who in latter times was born from a virgin womb.
He who gave the law upon Mount Sinai,
makes himself obedient to the ordinance of the law.
His mother has brought him to the priest and righteous elder, whose
    appointed lot it was to see Christ, the Lord.
Simeon, receiving him in his arms,
greatly rejoiced, crying aloud:
"Now, O Lord, let your servant depart in peace,
for mine eyes have seen your salvation.
The Lord of life and death,
and the Savior of our soul."

Byzantine Vespers

Responsory

Verse:

We magnify you, O Christ, Giver of life,
and we venerate your most pure Mother.

Response: Who, according to the law, has presented you today
into the temple of the Lord.

The Lord's Prayer

Blessing   Lord, our God,
today Christ, your only begotten Son,
is carried into the temple in the arms of his mother
where he is shown to the people of Israel
to whom he brings salvation.
Open our hearts to receive him,
that we may be enlightened by his presence,
and sanctified by his visitation.
Send your blessing upon this meal
which we partake with joy
in the fellowship we have
with the same Jesus, your divine Son. Amen.

February 3: SAINT BLAISE, BISHOP

(See Common for the Feasts of Pastors and Confessors, pages 152-153.)

February 5: SAINT AGATHA, VIRGIN AND MARTYR

Reading   The righteous person who searches for the nature of all things makes an admirable discovery: that everything is God's grace. Every being in the world, and the world itself, manifests the blessings and generosity of God (Philo).

Responsory

Verse: Agatha, joyful and enveloped in light,
walked to embrace martyrdom saying:

Response: Lead me, Lord Jesus, to your eternal glory.

The Lord's Prayer

Blessing   Blessed be you, Lord God.
You are the strength of the martyrs and the virgins

whom you clothe with your beauty.
May the intercession of Saint Agatha,
who with humble fidelity kept the faith until death,
make us worthy to receive your pardon and mercy.
Bless our daily bread and drink,
and do not let us forget
the needs of those who are poor and hungry.
We ask you this through Christ our Lord. Amen.

February 10: SAINT SCHOLASTICA, NUN

Reading   O how truly admirable are the merits of the blessed Scholastica! How great is the power of her tears, through which the saintly nun drew floods of water from the sunny skies. Therefore, let the faithful Christian people rejoice in the glory of the gracious virgin, Scholastica; but most of all, let the choir of virgins and nuns be glad celebrating the feast of her who, pouring forth her tears, entreated the Lord; and because she loved so much, she obtained greater power from him (Ancient Office of St. Scholastica).

Responsory

Verse: Arise in haste, my love, my dove,
my beautiful one.

Response: Come, and receive the crown
the Lord has prepared for you.

The Lord's Prayer

Blessing   We praise your name, Lord and God,
for you clothed the virgin Scholastica
with the virtue of innocence
and the splendor of your beauty.
During the course of a meal with her
   brother Benedict,
she wished to celebrate your praises
   with him,
and you granted her heart's desire.

Grant us also the joy to proclaim your praise,
as we share this nourishment
which you lovingly provide for us.
We ask you this, through Jesus, your Son. Amen.

February 11: OUR LADY OF LOURDES

(See Common for the Feasts of the Mother of God, page 148.)

February 14: SAINTS CYRIL AND METHODIUS, PASTORS

(See Common for the Feasts of Pastors and Confessors, pages 152-153.)

February 18: SAINT BERNADETTE SOUBIROUS, RELIGIOUS

Reading Don't I realize that the Blessed Virgin chose me because I was the most ignorant? If she had found anyone more ignorant than myself, she would have chosen her. The Blessed Virgin used me like a broom. What do you do with a broom when you have finished sweeping? You put it back in its place, behind the door (St. Bernadette).

Responsory

Verse: She is the wise and prudent virgin
whom the Lord found watching in prayer.

Response: St. Bernardette, pray for us to Christ, the Lord.

The Lord's Prayer

Blessing Glory be to you, Lord our God!
You are the protector of the poor
and the defense of the meek and humble.
In your mercy, you filled St. Bernadette
with the virtues of patience and charity,
so that in all things she might imitate
the life of Christ, her master and Lord.
With the help of her prayerful intercession
we ask you to bless our daily nourishment
that we may be properly renewed
and strengthened for your service. Amen.

February 22: THE CHAIR OF PETER, APOSTLE

Reading   When Jesus came out to the region of Caesarea Philippi he put this ques-
tion to his disciples, "Who do people say the Son of man is?" And they
said, "Some say John the Baptist, some Elijah, and others Jeremiah or
one of the prophets." "But you," he said, "who do you say I am?" Then
Simon Peter spoke up and said, "You are the Christ, the Son of the
living God." Jesus replied, "Simon son of Jonah, you are a blessed man!
Because it was no human agency that revealed this to you but my
Father in heaven. So I now say to you: You are Peter and on this rock I
will build my community" (Mt 16:13-18).

Responsory

Verse: Jesus asked Peter: "Simon son of John,
do you love me more than these other do?"

Response: And Peter replied "Lord, you know everything;
you know I love you."

The Lord's Prayer

Blessing   Lord Jesus Christ,
you have built your church
on the faith of Peter and the apostles.
Grant us, through their intercession,
to grow daily in faith and a deeper love of you.
Bless this meal we are about to partake,
as you blessed many times the meal of your disciples,
and may your presence in our midst
be a sign of the eternal joy to come. Amen.

February 23: SAINT POLYCARP, BISHOP AND MARTYR

Reading   As Polycarp entered the amphitheater, a voice from heaven said: "Be
strong Polycarp, and have courage." No one saw who was speaking,
but those of our people who were present heard the voice. The governor asked him: "Are you Polycarp?" and when he admitted he was, the
governor tried to persuade him to say "Caesar is Lord." "Swear by him
and I will let you go. Curse Christ!" But Polycarp answered: "For

eighty-six years I have been his servant and he has done me no wrong. How can I blaspheme against my King and Savior?" (*Acts of the Christian Martyrs*).

Responsory

Verse: I bless you, Lord God, because you
               have thought me worthy of this day and hour,

Response: to have a share among the number of martyrs
               in the cup of your Christ (St. Polycarp).

The Lord's Prayer

Blessing   God, our Father,
               you strengthened Saint Polycarp
               and asked him to share in the company of martyrs.
               Through his intercession we ask you
               to bless this meal and those who share it with us
               that we may serve you faithfully
               all the days of our lives. Amen.

MARCH

March 7: SAINTS PERPETUA AND FELICITY, MARTYRS

Reading   The day of their victory dawned, and they marched from the prison to the amphitheater joyfully as though they were going to heaven, with calm faces, trembling, if at all, with joy rather than fear. Perpetua went along with shining countenance and calm step, as the beloved of God, as the spouse of Christ, putting down everyone's stare by her own intense gaze. With them also was Felicity, glad that she had safely given birth so that now she could fight the beasts, going from one blood bath to another, from the midwife to the gladiator, ready to wash after childbirth in a second baptism (*Acts of Christian Martyrs*).

Responsory

Verse: The martyrs Perpetua and Felicity
         have washed their robes in the blood of the Lamb.

Response: And they were crowned
            with glory and honor by the Lord.

The Lord's Prayer

Blessing   Almighty Lord, eternal God,
           today we honor with joy the virtuous lives
           and glorious martyrdom of your saints, Perpetua and Felicity.
           May the example of their lives
           encourage us to greater fidelity in your service.
           Bestow your blessing on this food, we pray,
           and on that of your sons and daughters around the world.
           We ask this through Jesus Christ your Son. Amen.

March 17: SAINT PATRICK, BISHOP AND MONK

Reading   May the strength of God pilot us.
          May the power of God preserve us.
          May the wisdom of God instruct us.
          May the hand of God protect us.
          May the way of God direct us.
          May the shield of God defend us.
          May the host of God guard us
          against the snares of evil
          and the temptations of the world.
          May Christ be with us.
          Christ before us.
          Christ in us.
          Christ over us.
          May your salvation, O Lord,
          be always ours this day
          and forever more.

St. Patrick's Breastplate

Responsory

Verse: Blessed and wise, St. Patrick,
          you received your call from God
          to bring the faith to the people of Ireland.

Response: And because of your obedience
           you were granted the gift of miracles
           and of healing diseases.

The Lord's Prayer

Blessing   Grant us, Lord our God,
           the grace to follow the example of St. Patrick,
           not setting our hearts on earthly things
           but to love instead things heavenly.
           Bless our daily bread and drink
           that thus strengthened anew,
           we may continue to serve you faithfully.
           We ask you this in Jesus' name. Amen.

March 19:
SAINT JOSEPH, HUSBAND OF MARY

Reading   The purity that made you stand out
           and the simplicity and innocence that shone
               forth from you,
           O just and most holy Joseph,
           have delighted the hearts of the faithful
           and shown us the royal road to heaven.
           Wherefore the heavenly powers were amazed
           as they beheld the heights of your unsurpassing
               glory.
           We too, the faithful, sing a hymn to you:
           Glory to the one who honored you, O just man!
           Glory to the one who crowned you, O spouse of
               Mary!
           Glory to the one who chose, Holy Joseph,
           as the intercessor for our souls!
                              Byzantine Office

Responsory

Verse: God has chosen you to become the foster-father
          of his only begotten Son, and the ever-Virgin Mary was entrusted to you
          as a pure bride.

Response: Wherefore you received the choicest gifts
          of the Holy Spirit. O Holy Joseph, intercede
          for the salvation of our souls (Byzantine Office).

The Lord's Prayer

Blessing Blessed be you, God our Father,
          for in your ineffable mercy and wisdom
          you chose St. Joseph to be the watchful servant
          who protected and cared for the needs of Jesus and Mary.
          Grant us, through his loving intercession,
          the grace to be attentive
          to the needs of our brothers and sisters.
          Bless the food and drink at our table,
          and renew us in mind and body for your service.
          Through Christ our Lord. Amen.

March 21: THE DEATH OF SAINT BENEDICT, ABBOT

(See July 11, Feast of St. Benedict.)

March 25: THE ANNUNCIATION OF THE LORD

Reading   Wild air, World-Mothering air …
           Of her flesh he took flesh:
           He does take fresh and fresh,
           Through much the mystery now
           And makes, O marvelous!
           New Nazareth in us,
           Where she shall yet conceive
           Him, morning, noon and eve
           New Bethlehems, and he born
           There, evening, noon and morn.

                   Gerard Manley Hopkins

TABLE BLESSINGS

Responsory

Verse: The angel of the Lord brought good tidings to Mary

Response: and she conceived of the Holy Spirit.

The Lord's Prayer

Blessing   Today, a prelude of joy for the whole world,
           the dawn of our salvation,
           is announced by Gabriel to the Virgin Mary.
           Let us hasten to celebrate with gladness,
           the coming of Christ among us,
           who dwelt in the bosom of the Father before time began.
           We pray, O Lord, as once you came to dwell in Mary,
           that you come today to live among us,
           for you alone are the way,
           the truth, and the true life. Amen.

March 30: SAINT JOHN CLIMACUS, ABBOT

Reading   Someone discovered in his heart how beautiful humility is, and in his
           amazement he asked her to reveal her parent's name. Humility smiled,
           joyous and serene: "Why are you in such a rush to learn the name of my
           begetter? He has no name, nor will I reveal him to you until you have
           God for your possession. To whom be glory forever." Amen (St. John
           Climacus, *The Divine Ladder*).

Responsory

Verse: The Lord led you to the desert
           to be a guiding star,

Response: showing us by your example and teaching
           the way to heaven, O holy father and teacher John.

The Lord's Prayer

Blessing   We thank you, God of love,
           and we praise your holy name,
           for the example and teaching of John Climacus.
           For your sake he abandoned the false pleasures of the world,

and retired to the Sinai desert
to follow Christ through fasting, vigils, and constant prayer.
He practiced special love for the poor,
and the sick he healed in your name.
Bless, O Lord, the food and drink of your servants,
may it renew our strength to follow you 'til the end.
We ask you this through Christ your Son. Amen.

APRIL

April 2: SAINT MARY OF EGYPT, HERMITESS

Reading

The essential message of the life of St. Mary of Egypt would, therefore, seem to be the abiding conviction that we do not know, nor are we meant to know, into the mind of God and hence, we cannot judge his values. We are ever pursued by the parables which deny our capacity of judgment. We are accompanied by the thief on the cross and the washing of her Lord's feet by the sinner. Such not knowing must find its outlet and expression in the repentance found so proper to St. Mary. We do not know the value of any thought or of any action. And, so, we repent, from day to day and from year to year and from minute to minute. And, in repenting, we keep our eyes fixed on the Mother of God, in her tender solicitude for us, and we walk toward Christ, Judge and Savior (Sister Thecla, *The Life of Mary of Egypt*).

Responsory

Verse: With eagerness and love, O Mary,
you did run toward Christ,
thus abandoning your former way of sin.

Response: And being nourished in the untrodden wilderness,
you chastely fulfilled his divine commandments
(St. Andrew of Crete's Canon).

The Lord's Prayer

Blessing   Blessed be you God, our Father.
You call all your children to repentance
and to acceptance of the gospel.
We praise you Lord, for in Blessed Mary the Egyptian
you give us an example of true conversion.
For by the stream of her tears she watered the whole wilderness,
bringing forth the fruits of repentance.
By the ascetical practices of fasting and abstinence
she conquered the passions of body and soul.
By accepting the silence of the desert
and by constant prayer,
she choked the power of the evil one.
Bless, O Lord, this meal we share,
and grant that by following Mary of Egypt in the ways of repentance,
we may come into the presence of Christ, your Son,
in whom the angels rejoice forever. Amen.

April 21: SAINT ANSELM, BISHOP AND DOCTOR

Reading   Therefore, when you resolve upon or prepare to do anything of importance, you must ask yourselves: Does God approve my determination
to do this, or does he not? If your conscience answers you: I am certain
that God approves this desire of mine, that he is pleased with my intention, then whether you can or whether you cannot carry out your plan,
you should hold fast to your intention. But if your conscience warns
you that God does not wish you to persevere in your project, then you
must abandon it with all your might (Letter of St. Anselm to His
Spiritual Daughters).

Responsory

Verse: The saints will sing for joy in heaven's glory;

Response: radiant is their victory over human frailties.

The Lord's Prayer

Blessing   Praise be given to you, merciful God,
            for through the example and teaching of Saint Anselm
            you inspire us to follow Christ in our daily lives and work.
            By the intercession of his prayer,
            bless our food and drink provided
            by you to sustain us in our journey.
            Make us always grateful for all your mercies
            and ever mindful of the needs of others.
            Grant this through Christ our Lord. Amen.

April 25: SAINT MARK, EVANGELIST

(See Common for the Feasts of Apostles and Evangelists, page 150.)

April 29: SAINT CATHERINE OF SIENA, VIRGIN AND DOCTOR

Reading   You, O God, are a fire that takes away the coldness, illuminates the
           mind with its light, and causes me to know your truth. And I know that
           you are beauty and wisdom itself. The food of the angels, you give your-
           self to [us] in the fire of your love (St. Catherine of Siena).

Responsory

Verse: How beautiful you are, Catherine,
           virgin of Christ.

Response: Nothing can separate you
           from the love of the Son of God.

The Lord's Prayer

Blessing	Blessed be you, compassionate God,
	for by the power of your Holy Spirit
	you made your dwelling place
	in the heart of the chaste virgin Catherine.
	Help us, by her steadfast prayers,
	to live daily by the power of your grace
	and to remain worthy temples of your Spirit.
	As we gather around this table,
	we ask your blessing on our food
	and on that of all your sons and daughters.
	We ask this in Jesus' name. Amen.

MAY

May 1: SAINT JOSEPH, THE WORKER

(See Proper for March 19.)

May 2: SAINT ATHANASIUS, BISHOP

Reading   As there is one body of the Catholic church, and a command is given us in the sacred scriptures to preserve the bond of unity and peace, it is agreeable therefore, that we should write and signify to one another whatever is done by each of us individually; so that whether one member suffers or rejoices, we may either suffer and rejoice with one another (St. Athanasius).

Responsory

Verse: St. Athanasius proved himself
           a faithful and wise servant,

Response: therefore the Lord entrusted him
           the care of his flock.

The Lord's Prayer

Blessing   Lord God, you called St. Athanasius
            to be a defender of the faith,
            and a beacon of light to the Christian people.
            You made him a shepherd of the church
            so that the faithful may be taught the truth
            by his wisdom and the example of his life.
            Bless your flock, gathered around this table,
            and by the intercession of St. Athanasius' prayers,
            grant that this nourishment we partake in joy
            may be ever beneficial to our souls and bodies.
            This we ask through Christ our Lord. Amen.

May 3: SAINTS PHILIP AND JAMES, APOSTLES

(See Common for the Feasts of Apostles and Evangelists, page 150.)

May 14: SAINT MATHIAS, APOSTLE

(See Common for the Feasts of Apostles and Evangelists, page 150.)

May 15: SAINT PACHOMIUS, ABBOT

Reading   On an occasion, when a brother had sold some sandals at a higher price
than the one agreed upon, Pachomius sharply reproved him. "You have
done grievous wrong, because you have loved gain. Go quickly, now,
and return what was in excess of the price to those who paid you, and
then come back and repent your fault." This incident is indicative of
Pachomius' concern lest any breath of covetousness taint his monks; the
cloister was not to be a place for the amassing of riches. On the contrary,
the monastery's surplus supplies were to be distributed among the
poor. The monastery thus initiated a new approach in economic rela-
tions, and in this respect, too, it was to prove the seed of a new social
order (Walter Nigg, *Warrior of God: St. Pachomius and Cenobitism*).

Responsory

Verse: Your abundant tears
made the desert sprout and bloom.

Response: Holy Pachomius, pray to Christ God
that he may save our souls.

The Lord's Prayer

Blessing   Blessed be you, Lord God,
     on this day in which we celebrate
     the memory of the humble monk Pachomius.
     You inspired him to institute the monastic form of life
     as a way of following the gospel of Jesus Christ.
     Grant us, O God, by this prayerful intercession
     to share this meal in the joy of the saints,
     keeping always in mind
     the needs of the poor and the destitute.
     We ask this through Christ our Lord. Amen.

May 25: SAINT BEDE, THE VENERABLE

Reading   If it so pleases my maker, it is time for me to return to him who created me and formed me out of nothing when I did not exist. I have lived a long time and the righteous Judge has taken good care of me during my whole life. The time has come for my departure, and I long to die and be with Christ. My soul yearns to see Christ, my King, in all his glory (St. Bede).

Responsory

Verse: The person who obeys God's law
    and teaches others to do so,

Response: will be great in the kingdom of heaven.

The Lord's Prayer

Blessing   We praise your name, merciful God,
     for you have enlightened us, your children,
     with the learning and the teachings of St. Bede.
     With the help of his prayers,
     may we grow daily in wisdom
     and in the knowledge and love of you.
     Send your blessing upon this meal,
     which we are about to partake in Jesus' name,
     your Son and our Lord. Amen.

May 31: THE VISITATION

Reading   Having begotten God in her womb, the Virgin hastened to Elizabeth, whose child understood the greeting and rejoiced with leapings as with songs, crying to the Mother of God:

Rejoice, O flower of unwithering stem!
Rejoice, O gift of an incorruptible fruit!
Rejoice, O fountain of the source of life, the lover of humanity!
Rejoice, O Mother of the Son of God the Father!
Rejoice, O field, a harvest of mercy!
Rejoice, O banquet, a feast of purity!
Rejoice, O flower, a meadow of delights!
Rejoice, O guide, the harbor of souls!
Rejoice, O acceptable incense of prayers!
Rejoice, O purification of the universe!
Rejoice, O goodness of God toward the dead!
Rejoice, O boldness of dead toward God!
Rejoice, O unwedded bride!

Akathist Hymn

Responsory

Verse: When Elizabeth heard Mary's greeting, she said:

Response: "Who am I that the mother of my Lord
should come to me?"

The Lord's Prayer

Blessing   Blessed be you, God of mercy and compassion,
for you inspired Mary, the humble maiden of Nazareth,
to visit her cousin Elizabeth
and to assist her in her earthly needs.
Help us, that following Mary's example
we may remain always open
to the needs and sufferings of others.
Strengthen us with the nourishment of this meal,
and bring us one day
to love's eternal feast in your kingdom.
Through Christ our Lord. Amen.

June 1: SAINT JUSTIN, MARTYR

Reading   The prefect Rusticus asked: "You are a Christian, then?"
Justin said: "Yes, I am a Christian."
The prefect said to Justin: "You are called a learned man and think you
know what is true teaching. Listen: if you were scourged and be-headed,
are you convinced that you would go up to heaven?"

Justin said: "I hope that I shall enter God's house if I suffer in that way.
For I know that God's favor is stored up until the end of the whole
world for all who have lived good lives."

The prefect Rusticus said: "If you do not as I have commanded, you
will be tortured without mercy."

Justin said: "We hope to suffer torment for the sake of our Lord Jesus
Christ, and so be saved. For this will bring us salvation and confidence
as we stand before the more terrible and universal judgment seat of our
Lord Jesus Christ" (*Acts of Martyrdom of Saint Justin and his Companions*).

Responsory

Verse: In every sacrifice let us praise
the Creator of all things.

Response: Through his Son Jesus Christ
and through the Holy Spirit.

The Lord's Prayer

Blessing   All praise be given to you, Lord Jesus,
for the martyrdom of Saint Justin
and his companions who gave their lives for you.
Neither torture nor the fear of death
could turn them away from their abiding faith in you.
Through the intercession of the holy martyrs,
bless our daily bread and drink,
that thus strengthened anew,
we may continue to serve you faithfully. Amen.

June 9: SAINT EPHREM, MONK, DEACON, AND DOCTOR

Reading Make me worthy through your grace to attain to paradise's gift
     this treasure of perfumes, this storehouse of scents.
     My hunger takes delight in the breath of its fragrance,
     for its scent gives nourishment to all at all times,
     and whoever inhales it is overjoyed
     and forgets his earthly bread;
     this is the table of the kingdom—
     blessed is he who prepared it in Eden.

              Saint Ephrem, Hymns on Paradise

Responsory

Verse: Lord, do not deprive our souls
     of the spiritual vision of you.

Response: Nor our bodies of your warmth and sweetness
     (St. Ephrem).

The Lord's Prayer

Blessing Blessed are you,
     God of Light, God of Love,
     for you filled the mind and heart of Saint Ephrem
     with the outpouring of your Holy Spirit.
     Your Spirit inspired him to serve you faithfully
     and to sing daily the praises of your mysteries.
     As we gather around this table,
     we ask your blessing on our food and drink.
     May this food be a sign
     of our unity with you and our sisters and brothers,
     through the power of the Holy Spirit.
     We ask you this through Christ the Lord. Amen.

June 11: SAINT BARNABAS, APOSTLE

(See Common for the Feasts of Apostles and Evangelists, page 150.)

June 14: SAINT ELISHA, PROPHET

(See Common for the Feasts of Prophets, pages 149-150.)

June 24: BIRTH OF JOHN THE BAPTIST

Reading   The woman who had been barren be-
comes fertile and gives birth today to
the forerunner of Christ. He is the
greatest and the last of the prophets, for
standing in the waters of the Jordan
River, he placed his hands on Christ
whom all the prophets had announced,
and in so doing, he became a prophet
himself, a preacher and forerunner of
the Word of God. O blessed John,
prophet and forerunner of Christ, we
praise and honor you with love. For it is
you who announces the Lamb who is to
come, Christ, our glorious God and
King! We entreat you, intercede for us,
O holy prophet, that he may grant us
his great mercy (Byzantine Office).

Responsory

Verse: Your glorious birth saved your mother
from the shame of barrenness,

Response: and returned to your father the power of speech,
heralding the incarnation of the Son of God.

The Lord's Prayer

Blessing   May you ever be blessed, merciful God,
for you sent John the Baptist as forerunner,
to prepare in the desert a way for Christ, your Son.
Open our hearts to the power of his love,
so that it may steadily increase in us

and daily transform our lives.
Through the prayers of John the Baptist,
may your blessing descend upon this table,
so that in receiving new strength
we may continue to praise your name forever.
We ask this in Jesus' name. Amen.

June 27: SAINT CYRIL, PATRIARCH OF ALEXANDRIA

(See Common for the Feasts of Pastors and Confessors, pages 152-153.)

June 28: SAINT IRENAEUS, BISHOP AND MARTYR

Reading   The Word became the steward of the Father's grace for the advantage of
[humankind], for whose benefit he made such wonderful arrange-
ments. He revealed God to [humanity] and presented [humanity] to
God. ... Life in [humankind] is the glory of God; the life of [humanity]
is the vision of God (St. Irenaeus, *Treatise Against the Heresies*).

Responsory

Verse: Saint Irenaeus, true to his name,
made peace the object of his life,

Response: and he labored to preserve
the unity of the church.

The Lord's Prayer

Blessing   Almighty God,
you inspired Saint Irenaeus
to teach your divine truth faithfully,
and to preserve at all cost the bond of unity in your church.
May we follow after his example,
becoming ministers of peace and reconciliation
among all your people.
Bestow your blessing upon this nourishment,
and may we learn to share it willingly with the poor,
the hungry, and the dispossessed.
We ask this through Christ the Lord. Amen.

June 29: SAINTS PETER AND PAUL, APOSTLES

Reading   What songs of praise could be worthy of Peter and Paul?
           They are like two wings on which the knowledge of God
           spreads out to the far ends of the earth and soars aloft to heaven,
           two hands from which the gospel pours forth grace,
           two feet on which the doctrine of the truth travels about the world,
           two rivers of wisdom,
           two arms of the cross through which the merciful Christ,
           casts down the pride of demons.

                                                        Byzantine Office

Responsory

Verse: Rejoice, apostle Peter, so closely linked
           with your teacher, Christ, our God.

Response: Rejoice, O beloved Paul, preacher of the faith
           and teacher to the gentiles.

The Lord's Prayer

Blessing   We praise your name, God almighty,
           as we keep today a splendid festival,
           commemorating the martyrdom
           of your glorious apostles, Peter and Paul.
           By the merits of their prayers,
           strengthen us in that faith
           which is built on the solid foundation of the apostles.
           Bless the food and drink of your servants,
           and grant that this nourishment
           may help us persevere faithfully in your service.
           Through Christ the Lord. Amen.

July 3: SAINT THOMAS, APOSTLE

Reading   In a marvelous way God's mercy arranged that the disbelieving disciple, in touching the wounds of his master's body, should heal our wounds of disbelief. The disbelief of Thomas has done more for our faith than the faith of the other disciples. As he touches Christ and is won over to belief, every doubt is cast aside and our faith is strengthened. So the disciple who doubted, then felt Christ's wounds, became a witness to the reality of the resurrection (St. Gregory the Great).

Responsory

Verse: Thomas, disciple of Christ,
            filled with divine grace cried out:
Response: "You are my Lord and my God!"

The Lord's Prayer

Blessing   We bless you, God of all goodness,
            on this day in which we celebrate
            the feast day of the apostle Thomas.
            May the example of his faith
            lead us to a firm belief in Christ,
            whom Thomas acknowledged as Lord and God.
            Send your blessing upon this meal
            and upon all those who share it with us
            in the fellowship that we have in Jesus' name. Amen.

July 6: ISAIAH, THE PROPHET

(See Common for the Feasts of Prophets, pages 149-150.)

July 11: SAINT BENEDICT, ABBOT

Reading   Let us encompass ourselves with faith and
the practice of good works, and guided by
the gospel, tread the path he has cleared for
us. Thus may we deserve to see him, who
has called us into his kingdom (St. Benedict,
Prologue of *The Rule*).

Responsory

Verse: Saint Benedict, blessed in name and in grace,

Response: put all his trust in God
and preferred nothing to the love of Christ.

The Lord's Prayer

Blessing   We bless your name, ever-faithful God,
on this day in which we keep the memory
of our father in the faith, Saint Benedict.
You made him a master and guide
on the ways of monastic life,
so that his disciples may learn
to tread the path of the gospel of Christ.
Through the help of his prayers,
bless our daily food and drink
and grant that we may always
love Christ above all else. Amen.

July 16: OUR LADY OF MOUNT CARMEL

(See Common for the Feasts of the Mother of God, pages 148-149.)

July 20: ELIJAH, PROPHET

(See Common for the Feasts of Prophets, pages 149-150.)

July 22: SAINT MARY MAGDALENE

Reading   We should reflect on Mary's attitude and the great love she felt for Christ; for though the disciples had left the tomb, she remained. She was still seeking the one she had not found, and while she sought she wept; burning with the fire of love, she longed for him whom she thought had been taken away. And so it happened that the woman who stayed behind to seek Christ was the only one to see him. She immediately calls him *"rabboni,"* that is to say, teacher, because the one whom she sought outwardly was the one who inwardly taught her to keep on searching (St. Gregory the Great).

Responsory

Verse: How blessed are you, Mary Magdalene, apostle to the apostles,

Response: for you were the first to proclaim that the Lord had truly risen.

The Lord's Prayer

Blessing   Holy and immortal God, we bless your name on this day on which we celebrate the life of your servant, Mary Magdalene. You chose her to be the first witness to the resurrection of Christ, and sent her later to announce the good tidings to the disciples. May her prayers merit us to proclaim daily the joyful news of Christ's resurrection. Bestow your blessing on this food, we pray, and on that of all your sons and daughters around the world. We ask this in Jesus' name. Amen.

July 25: SAINT JAMES, APOSTLE

(See Common for the Feasts of Apostles and Evangelists, page 150.)

July 26: SAINTS JOACHIM AND ANN, PARENTS OF MARY

Reading   A great joy has shone upon us
           from the two just ones, Joachim
           and Ann; and this joy is the most
           honorable Virgin Mary who is
           chosen to become a temple of the
           living God, and who alone will be
           recognized as the Mother of God.
           Through the intercession of your
           holy ancestors, O Christ our God,
           send down peace and mercy upon
           the world (Byzantine Office).

Responsory

Verse: Joachim and Ann worshipped God
           day and night,

Response: waiting for the day that God would
           come to save his people.

The Lord's Prayer

Blessing   Ever-mighty Lord,
           God of our fathers and mothers,
           You present the parenthood of Joachim and Ann as a model.
           You chose them to become the parents of Mary,
           and the glorious ancestors of your eternal Son.
           May their prayers help us to look forward in joyful expectation,
           to the eternal banquet of heaven,
           when Christ will be all in all. Amen.

AUGUST

August 1:
SAINT ALPHONSUS LIGUORI, BISHOP AND FOUNDER

Reading Since God knew that [we] are enticed by favors, he wished to bind [us] to his love by means of gifts: "I want to catch them with the snares, those chains of love in which they allow themselves to be entrapped, so that they will love me." And all the gifts God bestowed on [us] were given to that end. He gave [us] a soul, made in his likeness … and a body equipped with the senses; it was for [us] that he created heaven and earth and such an abundance of things (St. Alphonsus Liguori).

Responsory

Verse: For you bless the righteous, O Lord;

Response: you cover them with favor as with a shield (Ps 5:12).

The Lord's Prayer

Blessing You are blessed, Lord our God,
for you introduce again and again
new examples of gospel living in your church.
Today, as we celebrate the memory of Saint Alphonsus,
we ask you to grant us the zeal for souls
which he possessed in so large a measure.
Bless our daily bread and drink,
and all those seated at this table,
and lead us all to the joys of the promised kingdom. Amen.

August 4: SAINT JOHN-MARIE VIANNEY, PRIEST

Reading My children, your heart is small, but prayer enlarges it and makes it capable of loving God. Prayer is a foretaste of heaven, a passing glimpse into paradise. It never leaves us without sweetness. It is a honey which comes down into the soul and sweetens everything. Sorrow melts away before a well-offered prayer, like snow before the sun (St. John-Marie Vianney).

Responsory

Verse: Every day I will bless you,
            and praise your name forever and ever.

Response: Great is the Lord, and greatly to be praised;
            his greatness is unsearchable (Ps 145:2-3).

The Lord's Prayer

Blessing   Blessed be you, Lord, God of all goodness,
            for by the exemplary life of John-Marie Vianney
            you encourage us to follow you
            by sincere attempts to live the gospel.
            He was a faithful priest-servant,
            totally devoted to you and to the flock he ministered.
            May his example and doctrine inspire us
            to bear in our lives fruits of true holiness.
            Bless the food and drink set at this table,
            may they sustain us in our journey.
            We ask you this through Christ our Lord. Amen.

August 6:
THE TRANSFIGURATION

Reading

You were transfigured on Mount Tabor,
    O Jesus,
and a shining cloud, spread like a tent,
covered the apostles with your glory.
Whereupon their gaze fell to the ground,
for they could not bear to look upon the
    brightness
of the unapproachable glory of your face.
O Savior Christ, you are God without
    beginning or end,
as you once have shone upon your
    disciples
the light of your glory,
today give new life and light to our im-
    mortal souls.

                      Byzantine Office

Responsory

Verse: We magnify you, O Christ, the giver of life,

Response: and we venerate your all-glorious transfiguration
             in the holy mountain (Byzantine Office).

The Lord's Prayer

Blessing

We praise your glory, God of all mercy,
for you have revealed to us the splendor of your divinity
in the transfigured face of Christ, your Son.
The light of Christ's transfiguration
fills the world with infinite joy.
As happy partakers of this joy today,
we ask you to bless our meal
which we receive from your bounty,
and to make of us always
lovers of your heavenly glory.
Through Jesus Christ our Lord. Amen.

August 8: SAINT DOMINIC, FOUNDER

Reading   Dominic manifested himself everywhere as a man of the gospel, in word and in deeds. During the day, no one mixed more than he did in the society of his brethren or his companions along the road, no one was more joyous. But in the night, no one was more eager to watch, to pray, and make supplication in all possible ways. His tears pervaded the evening and his joy the morning. He gave the day to his neighbor and the night to God, knowing that God assigns his mercy to the day and his song to the night (Blessed Jordan of Saxony).

Responsory

Verse: The Lord said to his disciples:
You are the salt of the earth;

Response: but if the salt loses its strength,
what shall it be salted with?

The Lord's Prayer

Blessing   We praise your name, Lord our God,
on this day in which we keep the memory of St. Dominic.
He preached the truth of the gospel,
both by word and by the example of his life.
May his prayerful intercession help us
to hold fast to this truth in our daily lives.
Send your blessing upon this food
which we are about to partake
in the peace and joy of Christ our Lord. Amen.

August 10: SAINT LAWRENCE, DEACON AND MARTYR

Reading   As you have often heard, Lawrence was a deacon of the church of Rome. There he ministered the sacred blood of Christ; there for the sake of Christ's name he poured out his own blood. St. John the Apostle was evidently teaching us about the mystery of the Lord's supper when he wrote: just as Christ laid down his life for us, so we ought to lay down our lives for the brethren. My brethren, Lawrence understood this and, understanding, he acted on it. In his life he loved Christ; in his death he followed in his footsteps (St. Augustine).

Responsory

Verse: The blessed Lawrence cried out:
            "I worship my God and serve him alone."

Response: "God is my rock; I take refuge in him."

The Lord's Prayer

Blessing   Blessed be you, Lord God,
            for you made the deacon Lawrence
            a model of dedication and service to the poor,
            and you crowned his life at the end with the glory of martyrdom.
            Help us by following his example,
            to always be attentive to the needs of our brothers and sisters.
            Bless this meal we share in your presence,
            may it nourish us and refresh us for your service.
            We ask this in Jesus' name. Amen.

August 11: SAINT CLARE, ABBESS

Reading   In this life, Francis and Clare had such great and warm human hearts, and such God-enlightened souls that even reading their story makes us feel near them. Now, in their closeness to God, they are still nearer to all who need them, and they can light the love of Christ in other hearts. There are no barriers left for them, and they can help us to break down those that are the cause of so much of our misery. As Clare said to Agnes, so we can say to her: "Pray that by the help of God we may be enabled to call upon the mercy of Jesus Christ and with you to enjoy this blessedness in the Beatific Vision (Nesta de Robeck, *St. Clare of Assisi*).

Responsory

Verse: Love one another in the charity of Christ;

Response: and let the love you have inwardly
           be manifested outwardly by your works
           (*The Testament of St. Clare*).

The Lord's Prayer

Blessing   Lord, almighty God,
           you called St. Clare and her companions
           to follow Christ, your Son, by embracing
           the poverty and simplicity of the gospel.
           Today, as we celebrate her feast day,
           we ask you to grant us the grace
           to imitate Clare's fidelity and obedience
           to all the precepts of the Lord.
           Bless our food and bless our drink,
           which we partake of in the joy of knowing
           that all perfect gifts come from you. Amen.

August 15: THE ASSUMPTION

Reading   Come, O peoples, from all the ends
of the earth,
and together, let us praise
the glorious Assumption of the
Mother of God:
for she has delivered her spotless
soul
into the hands of her Son.
Therefore the world,
restored to life by her holy
dormition,
in radiant joy celebrates this feast
with psalms and hymns and spiritual songs,
together with the angels and
apostles.
With her all things are filled with
joy
and she bestows great mercy
upon us.

                           Byzantine Office

Responsory

Verse: Neither the tomb nor death
had power over the Mother of God,

Response: who is ever watchful in her prayers
and in whose intercession lies our unfailing hope
(Byzantine Office).

The Lord's Prayer

Blessing   Almighty, eternal God,
we praise you and give you thanks
on this day in which the Mother of your Son
was carried from earth to heaven.
May she never cease to intercede for us,
obtaining peace and great mercy for our world.

And grant, O Lord, your blessing to this nourishment
which we receive from your bounty.
We ask this through Christ our Lord. Amen.

August 20: SAINT BERNARD OF CLAIRVAUX, ABBOT

Reading   O true noon-day
When warmth and light are at
    their peak,
and the sun at its zenith
and no shadows fall;
when stagnant waters dry up
and their fetid odors disperse.
O never-ending solstice
when daylight lasts forever.
O noon-day light,
marked with the mildness of
    spring,
stamped with summer's bold
    beauty,
enriched with autumn's fruit
and—lest I seem to forget—
calm with winter's rest from toil.

St. Bernard,
Sermon on the Song of Songs

Responsory

Verse: Blessed Bernard, friend of
Christ the Bridegroom,

Response: your monastic life illuminates the Christian people
with the light of true faith and doctrine.

The Lord's Prayer

Blessing   Lord God, heavenly Father,
today you fill your church with joy
as we celebrate the memory of St. Bernard,
whose heart was filled with love for you,

and for his brothers and sisters.
May he obtain for us the grace
of this deep and steadfast love,
which is the sole reason for our Christian lives.
Glory to you, O Lord,
for being the provider of food for our bodies
and the true nourishment of our souls. Amen.

August 22: THE QUEENSHIP OF MARY

(See Common for the Feasts of the Mother of God, pages 148-149, or use Proper for the Feast of the Assumption of Mary, August 15, whose octave we celebrate today.)

August 24: SAINT BARTHOLOMEW, APOSTLE

(See Common for the Feasts of Apostles and Evangelists, page 150.)

August 25: SAINT LOUIS, KING OF FRANCE

Reading   Be kindhearted to the poor, the unfortunate and the afflicted. Give them as much help and consolation as you can. Thank God for all his benefits he has bestowed upon you, that you may be worthy to receive greater. Be just to your subjects, swaying neither to right nor left, but holding the line of justice. Always side with the poor rather than with the rich, until you are certain of the truth (St. Louis, *Spiritual Testament to His Son*).

Responsory

Verse: Saint Louis did what was pleasing
in the sight of the Lord;

Response: among all kings none could compare with him.

The Lord's Prayer

Blessing   We glorify you, eternal God,
            for you raised Saint Louis
            from the cares of earthly rule
            to the glory of your heavenly kingdom.
            Through his intercession
            we ask you to bless our daily food and drink,
            and to not let us forget the needs
            of those who are poor and hungry.
            We ask you this through Christ our Lord. Amen.

August 28: SAINT AUGUSTINE, BISHOP

Reading   Late have I loved you, O Beauty ever ancient, ever new, late have I
           loved you! You were within me, but I was outside, and it was there that
           I searched for you. In my unloveliness I plunged into the lovely things
           which you created. You were with me, but I was not with you. Created
           things kept me from you; yet if they had not been in you they would
           not have been at all. You called, you shouted, and you broke through
           my deafness. You flashed, you shone, and you dispelled my blindness.
           You breathed your fragrance on me; I drew in breath and now I pant for
           you. I have tasted you, now I hunger and thirst for more. You touched
           me, and I burned for your peace (St. Augustine, *Confessions*).

Responsory

Verse: O Lord, you made us for yourself;

Response: our hearts are restless until they rest in you
            (St. Augustine).

The Lord's Prayer

Blessing   O Lord, almighty God,
            beauty ever ancient, yet ever new,
            you renew daily your Christian people
            by the power of the same Spirit,
            who filled St. Augustine
            with depths of wisdom and love.
            Through the power of the Holy Spirit,
            may we be renewed in body and soul

by this nourishment which comes from your hands,
so that we may serve you faithfully,
and love you above all things
all the days of our lives.
We ask this through Jesus, your Son. Amen.

August 29:
BEHEADING OF SAINT JOHN THE BAPTIST, MARTYR

(See Proper for June 24, or see the Common for the Feasts of Martyrs, page 151.)

SEPTEMBER

September 4: MOSES, PATRIARCH AND PROPHET

(See Common for the Feasts of Prophets, pages 149-150.)

September 8: THE BIRTH OF MARY

Reading   Joachim and Ann rejoice in great manner,
having brought into the world the Mother of God,
the first fruit of our salvation.
With them we keep a holy festival today,
blessing the pure maiden, born of the root of Jesse.
She is the glory of the prophets and the daughter of David.
And, in time, by giving birth to Christ,
she overthrows the curse of Adam that weighed upon us.

Byzantine Office

Responsory

Verse: Today grace begins to bear its first fruits;

Response: today the winds that blow
bring tidings of salvation.

The Lord's Prayer

Blessing   Blessed be you, O God, the most high,
for through the birth of the Mother of God
you announced to the whole world
the good tidings of our salvation.
Mary is the true "bridge of life"
who contributes to our deliverance
by giving birth in time to Christ, our Savior.
By the intercession of her prayers we ask you:
bless our daily bread and drink,
so that through this nourishment
we may be renewed for your service.
We ask this through Jesus,
Son of God and Son of Mary. Amen.

September 13: SAINT JOHN CHRYSOSTOM, BISHOP

Reading   Do you wish to honor Christ's body? Then do not scorn him in his nakedness, nor honor him here in the church with silken garments while neglecting him outside where he is cold and naked. The rich man is not he who is in possession of much, but one who gives much (St. John Chrysostom).

Responsory

Verse: Blessed John Chrysostom,
grace shines forth from your mouth,

Response: and like a torch it has enlightened the universe.

The Lord's Prayer

Blessing   Blessed be you, most holy and triune God,
for you have given us in St. John Chrysostom
a wise teacher to teach us the worship
of the one God in a Trinity of Persons.
By the help of his prayers we beseech you to bless
this meal we are about to partake,
and make us always mindful of the needs of others. Amen.

September 14: THE EXALTATION OF THE HOLY CROSS

Reading   The cross is raised on high,
            and urges all creation to sing the praises
            of the blessed passion of him who was lifted high upon it.
            For it was there that he snatched our slayer,
            and brought the dead to life again:
            and in his exceeding goodness and compassion
            he restored life to us,
            counting us worthy to be citizens of heaven.
            Therefore, let us exalt his name,
            and rejoicing, let us magnify his loving kindness.

                                        Byzantine Office

Responsory

Verse: As we behold the wood of the cross
            exalted on high today,

Response: let us glorify Christ who in his goodness
            was crucified upon it in the flesh
            (Byzantine Office).

The Lord's Prayer

Blessing   Lord Jesus Christ,
            by your suffering and death on the cross
            you make us aware of your immense love for us.
            May your holy cross be always a sign
            of your unfailing protection in our lives.
            Bestow your blessing upon the food present at this table,
            that it may nourish us for your service. Amen.

September 15: SAINT CATHERINE OF GENOA, WIDOW

Reading   When I eat or drink, move or stand still, speak or keep silent, sleep or
            wake, see, hear, or think; whether I am in church, at home, or in the
            street, in bad health or good, dying or not dying, at every hour and mo-
            ment of my life, I wish all to be in God. I wish to be unable to wish or

do or think or speak anything that is not completely God's will; and the part of me which would oppose this I would wish to be turned into dust and scattered in the wind (St. Catherine of Genoa).

Responsory

Verse: The Lord is merciful and gracious,

Response: slow to anger and abounding in steadfast love
           (Ps 103:8).

The Lord's Prayer

Blessing   Lord, our God,
           we praise your holy name
           as we celebrate the memory and the life
           of your servant, Catherine of Genoa.
           For your sake, she distributed her earthly wealth to the poor,
           and strived in all things to remain united to Christ, your Son.
           Through the intercession of her prayers
           we ask you to bless this food and this drink
           which your loving providence provides for our sustenance.
           We ask this through Christ our Lord. Amen.

September 17: SAINT HILDEGARD OF BINGEN, ABBESS

Reading   As the hart pants after the water-brook, so my soul pants after you, O God! (Ps 41:2). Therefore, I will skip over the mountains and hills, and bypass the sweet weakness of this transitory life, and with pure heart regard only the Fountain of living water. For he is full of immeasurable glory, with whose sweetness no one can ever be sated (St. Hildegard of Bingen, *Scivias*).

Responsory

Verse: O holy Hildegard, graced by the Holy Spirit,
         you were commanded to write,

Response: to tell the people of God
            how to enter the kingdom of heaven.

The Lord's Prayer

Blessing   Almighty, eternal God,
           you made your grace shine forth like fire
           from the lips of your servant Hildegard
           in order to enlighten all creation.
           By the power of the Holy Spirit
           she saw and heard
           what others could not see or perceive.
           Guided by her example and teaching,
           and nourished by this meal which comes from your hands,
           lead us firmly on the path of that kingdom
           where Jesus is Lord, forever and ever. Amen.

September 21: SAINT MATTHEW, APOSTLE

Reading   As Jesus was walking on from there he saw a man named Matthew sit-
          ting at the tax office, and he said to him, "Follow me." And he got up
          and followed him (Mt 9:9).

Responsory

Verse: Search me, O God, and know my heart;
         test me and know my thoughts.

Response: See if there is any wicked way in me,
            and lead me in the way everlasting (Ps 139:23-24).

The Lord's Prayer

Blessing   We praise your name, O Lord,
           God of mercy and compassion,
           as we celebrate the life, the teaching, and the martyrdom
           of your apostle Matthew

who left all things behind in order to follow you.
May we also be strengthened in our resolve to follow your gospel.
Bless this meal which we are about to share,
in the fellowship we have in your name. Amen.

September 27: SAINT VINCENT DE PAUL

Reading Extend mercy toward others, so that there is no one in need whom we meet without helping. For what hope is there for us if God should withdraw his mercy from us? (St. Vincent de Paul).

Responsory

Verse: Show us your steadfast love, O Lord,

Response: and grant us your salvation (Ps 85:7).

The Lord's Prayer

Blessing Be present at our table, Lord;
be here and everywhere adored.
These creatures bless,
and grant that we may feast
in paradise with thee. Amen.
John Wesley

September 29: MICHAEL, GABRIEL, AND RAPHAEL, ARCHANGELS

Reading Angels are messengers of God, or powers stemming from God, "ministering spirits" (Heb 1:14), who are often presented under human form in the Bible. They give concrete form to God's goodness, these great and good forces which work with us in this creation. … The Bible presents them as fully involved in our history of salvation in

Christ. And everything that is said about them in the Bible proclaims the marvelous truth: that God is concerned for us in a thousand ways.

The names of the angels tell us this. Gabriel means "strength of God"; Raphael, "God's healing"; Michael, "who is like God?" (*A New Catechism*).

Responsory

Verse: No evil shall befall you,
            no scourge come near your tent.

Response: For he will command his angels concerning you
            to guard you in all your ways (Ps 91:10-11).

The Lord's Prayer

Blessing   Holy God, maker of all,
            you have created the angels Michael, Gabriel, and Raphael
            to be servants of your glory
            and messengers of your faithful love for us.
            As they minister to us in your name
            with compassion and goodness,
            may we be filled with renewed fervor
            to accomplish the task you give us to do on earth.
            And thus merit their continual protection
            and the grace to be partakers one day
            of your heavenly banquet. Amen.

September 30: SAINT JEROME, PRIEST AND DOCTOR

Reading   To be a Christian is the greatest thing, not merely to seem one. And somehow or other those please the world most who please Christ least (St. Jerome).

Responsory

Verse: Deal bountifully with your servant,
            so that I may live and observe your word.

Response: Open my eyes, so that I may behold
            wondrous things out of your law (Ps 119:17-18).

The Lord's Prayer

Blessing   We praise your name, Lord God,
for you filled with the Holy Spirit
our father in the faith, St. Jerome.
Your Spirit gave him a taste
for the study of sacred scripture,
that he in turn may instruct your people
and enlighten the church throughout the ages.
Grant us that we may be daily nourished
by the wisdom of your word,
and the bread that you provide at this table,
and thus grow ever closer to you.
We ask you this through Christ your Son. Amen.

OCTOBER

October 1: SAINT THÉRÈSE OF THE CHILD JESUS, NUN

Reading   If a wild flower could talk, I imagine that it would tell us quite candidly about all God has done for it; there would be no point in hushing up his gifts to it, out of mock humility, and pretending that it was ugly, that it had no smell, that the sun had robbed it of its bloom, or the wind broken its stem, knowing that all that wasn't true. Anyhow, this isn't going to be the autobiography of a flower like that. On the contrary, I'm delighted to be able to put them on the record, the favors the Lord has shown to me, all quite undeserved (St. Thérèse of the Child Jesus, *Autobiography*).

Responsory

Verse: Truly I say to you, unless you change your lives
and become like little children,

Response: you will not enter the kingdom of heaven.

The Lord's Prayer

Blessing   We bless you, heavenly Father,
            on this feast of Saint Thérèse. For love of you,
            she was willing to become as a little child,
            allowing you to lead her through the narrow ways of the gospel.
            Through her intercession,
            bless the food and the drink at this table,
            and grant that we may be spiritually filled
            with the good things of your house.
            Through Christ our Lord.
            Amen.

October 2: THE GUARDIAN ANGELS

Reading   They come, God's messengers of love,
            they come from realms of peace above,
            from homes of never-fading light,
            from blessful mansions ever bright.
            Lord, to us the zeal of angels give,
            with love to serve you while we live;
            To us an angel-guard supply,
            when on the bed of death we lie.

                                        Robert Campbell

Responsory

Verse: God gave his angels charge over us,

Response: to protect us in all our ways.

The Lord's Prayer

Blessing   Almighty God, our creator,
            we unite with the choir of angels
            to sing your praises daily.
            And today, we give you thanks
            for giving the angels to us,
            as messengers of your mysteries
            and as protectors of our bodies and souls.
            Grant us to share this meal
            in peace, joy, and thanksgiving,

being always mindful
of the unfailing protection of our guardian angels.
We ask you this, through Christ, our Lord.
Amen.

October 4: SAINT FRANCIS OF ASSISI, FOUNDER

Reading   The gospel orders us, too, to love our
neighbors as ourself. Let us then do
good to our brethren instead of doing
evil; if it is our business to judge, let us
judge with mercy; if our function is to
command, let us exercise our powers
without indulgence, considering ourselves as the servants of others; if it be
our role to obey, let us do so with
humility, unless what is commanded to
us is a sin; let us avoid excess at table;
let us practice penance, let us give
generously to the poor; and finally let
us be simple, modest, and pure rather
than prudent and wise according to the
flesh (St. Francis of Assisi).

Responsory

Verse: Francis, while on earth was a poor and lowly man.

Response: Today he enters heaven rich in God's favor,
greeted with songs of rejoicing.

The Lord's Prayer

Blessing   Lord Jesus Christ,
you gave us in Saint Francis
a perfect example of gospel living.
Today, as we celebrate the gift of his life
help us to walk in his footsteps,
in peace and joy,
following the path your gospel has traced for us.

Bless the food spread upon this table,
and lead us all to the eternal banquet of heaven.
Amen.

October 7: OUR LADY OF THE ROSARY

(See Common for the Feasts of the Mother of God, pages 148-149.)

October 9: ABRAHAM, PATRIARCH

(See Common for the Feasts of Prophets, page 149-150.)

October 15:
SAINT TERESA OF AVILA,
NUN AND FOUNDRESS

Reading   We need no wings to go in search
of him,
but have only to find a place
where we can be alone
and look upon him present within
us.

                 St. Teresa of Avila

Responsory

Verse: What a joy it is to be near my
God,

Response: and to put daily all my trust in
the Lord.

The Lord's Prayer

Blessing   Blessed be you, God of our fathers and mothers,
for you filled the heart of Saint Teresa
with zeal for your service, and an ardent love of souls.
Inspired by her holy teachings, grant us the grace
to walk daily the way of perfection and holiness.

Bless this food and drink of your servants,
for you alone are holy forever and ever.
Amen.

October 17:
SAINT IGNATIUS OF ANTIOCH, BISHOP AND MARTYR

Reading   I am God's wheat; may I be ground by the teeth of wild beasts that I
            may become the pure bread of Christ. My passions have been crucified,
            and there is not in me any sensuous fire, but a spring rising up in me
            and murmuring within me: "Come to the Father" (St. Ignatius).

Responsory

Verse: Let us drink water with joy,

Response: from the spring of the Savior (Roman Liturgy).

The Lord's Prayer

Blessing   All-powerful and ever-living God,
            we praise your holy name
            for the witness of the bishop and martyr,
            Ignatius of Antioch.
            He offered himself as grain to be ground
            by the teeth of wild beasts,
            and thus presented his life to you
            as pure bread to be offered in sacrifice.
            Accept today, through the intercession of your saint,
            the humble tribute of our lives,
            and grant that through the partaking of this meal
            we may be properly renewed for your service.
            We ask this through Christ our Lord.
            Amen.

October 18: SAINT LUKE, EVANGELIST

(See Common for the Feasts of Apostles and Evangelists, page 150.)

October 28: SAINTS SIMEON AND JUDE, APOSTLES

(See Common for the Feasts of Apostles and Evangelists, page 150.)

NOVEMBER

November 1: ALL SAINTS

Reading   The saints are real and their presence on earth, inside the Mystery of Christ, remains an objective reality. The Mother of God, on earth and in heaven, is close and familiar but ever beyond our comprehension unless she, herself, gives a direct command. The Mother of God and the Saints are our friends and will help us, if we do not interfere too much ourselves; so on earth we need never be alone, and, in them, we are promised a personal heaven. And, in them, we see the true measure of success which alone is our comfort in the work of love (*Mother Maria, Her Life in Letters*).

Responsory

Verse: God himself is the eternal reward of all the saints:

Response: Therefore let them praise and glorify God's name.

The Lord's Prayer

Blessing   Blessed are you, ever-living God,
             in the saintly men and women
             of every time and place,
             who today share in the glory of your kingdom.
             You knit them together in a communion of love,
             in the fellowship of the church,
             which is the body of Christ, your Son.
             Through the merits of their prayerful intercession,
             may your blessing descend upon this meal
             and upon those who partake of it.

And may we come one day to the banquet table of heaven,
which you have prepared for all those who truly love you.
We ask you this through Christ our Lord.
Amen.

November 11: SAINT MARTIN OF TOURS, MONK AND BISHOP

Reading   No one ever saw [Martin] enraged or excited, or lamenting, or laughing;
he was always one and the same: displaying a kind of heavenly happiness in his countenance, he seemed to have passed the ordinary limits
of human nature. Never was there any word on his lips but Christ, and
never was there a feeling in his heart except piety, peace, and tender
mercy. Frequently, too, he used to weep for the sins of those who
showed themselves his revilers—those who, as he led his retired monastic life, slandered him with poisoned tongue and a viper's mouth
(Sulpitius Severus, *Life of Saint Martin*).

Responsory

Verse: Saint Martin loved God's people
and always prayed for them.

Response: He spoke only of Christ,
of his peace and his mercy.

The Lord's Prayer

Blessing   Lord God, source of all that is good,
            we praise your holy name on this day
            in which we celebrate the memory
            of your faithful servant, Martin of Tours.
            By the example of his life,
            renew in us the desire to follow daily
            in the footsteps of Christ, your Son.
            Bless this nourishment,
            which we receive from your bounty.
            May it strengthen us for your service.
            We ask this through Christ our Lord.
            Amen.

November 16: SAINT GERTRUDE THE GREAT, NUN

Reading   I vow obedience, to you, my God, because your fatherly charity allures
           me, your loving kindness and gentleness attract me. In observing your
           will, I tie myself to you because clinging to you is lovable above every-
           thing (St. Gertrude the Great).

Responsory

Verse: The Lord loved Gertrude with an everlasting love;

Response: from her childhood, he drew her to himself.

The Lord's Prayer

Blessing   All praise to you, God of love and mercy,
            for you poured your Holy Spirit into the heart of Saint Gertrude
            and filled her with the ineffable delights of your divine love.
            With the help of her prayerful intercession,
            we ask you today for the outpouring of your Spirit
            into the emptiness of our hearts,
            that we may learn to love you above all things.
            Bestow your blessing upon our table, we pray,
            and on all those dear to us,
            and make us always mindful of the needs of others.
            We ask this through Christ, our Lord and God.
            Amen.

November 21: THE PRESENTATION OF MARY

Reading

Today let the faithful dance for joy,
singing to the Lord with psalms and
    hymns,
venerating his hallowed tabernacle,
    the living ark,
that contained the Word who cannot
    be contained.
For she, a young child in the flesh,
is offered in wondrous fashion to the
    Lord in his temple,
and Zechariah, the great high priest,
rejoicing receives her who is to be the
    dwelling place of God.

Byzantine Vespers

Responsory

Verse: Today Joachim and Ann fulfill their promise,

Response: offering their child as a sacrifice
in the house of God.

The Lord's Prayer

Blessing

Blessed are you, God of peace,
and of infinite mercy.
Today we celebrate the solemn feast
of the entrance of Mary into the temple.
There she is offered to you by her parents
and in turn she is fed by your divine grace.
Through her loving intercession,
we ask your blessing upon this table
and upon the nourishment we are about to receive.
And grant that we may always be gladdened
by the unfailing protection of the Mother of God.
We ask this through Christ, our Savior.
Amen.

November 27: OUR LADY OF THE MIRACULOUS MEDAL

(See Common for the Feasts of the Mother of God, pages 148-149.)

November 30: SAINT ANDREW, APOSTLE

Reading   Let us praise Saint Andrew for his courage,
the first-called among the apostles
and brother of Peter, their leader,
for in like manner as he drew his brother to
    Christ,
he is crying out to us:
"Come, for we have found the one the world
    desires!"

                  Byzantine Office

Responsory

Verse: Saint Andrew, intercede for us with the
master of all,

Response: that he may grant peace to the world.

The Lord's Prayer

Blessing   We praise you, Lord Jesus Christ,
for the faith of your apostle Andrew,
who as soon as he heard your calling,
left aside the nets which were his livelihood
and without hesitation, went to follow you.
May we also be ever ready
to leave our worldly cares behind,
and promptly follow you at all times.
Bless the food and drink of your servants
as you blessed many times that of your apostles,
for you alone are all holy unto ages of ages.
Amen.

December 6: SAINT NICHOLAS, BISHOP

Reading   Saint Nicholas, the most human of saints, was always ready to help where need existed. By his very humanity, the saint reflected popular hopes and fears. He changed because human needs changed. He is what he is today, as Santa Claus, because we yearn for a season of altruism, childlike innocence, and "Peace on earth." We look for the visitation of a kindly familiar figure who makes children of us all (Martin Eben, *Saint Nicholas, Life and Legend*).

Responsory

Verse: Holy Father Nicholas, your holiness of life
was set before your flock as a rule of faith.

Response: You were a living example of meekness,
temperance, humility, and poverty of spirit.

The Lord's Prayer

Blessing   Almighty and merciful God,
in your love for us, your children,
you inspired the Bishop Nicholas
to deeds of kindness and relief for the poor.
By the help of his prayers
keep us safe from grief and danger,
and guide us daily on the path of our eternal salvation.
Bless us and these your gifts at the table,
and grant that through the breaking of bread together,
we may grow closer to you and to one another.
We ask this in Jesus' name.
Amen.

December 7: SAINT AMBROSE, BISHOP

(See Common for the Feasts of Pastors and Confessors, pages 152-153.)

December 8: THE IMMACULATE CONCEPTION

Reading   Today the universe rejoices,
for Ann has conceived the Mother
   of God,
in a manner provided by God
   himself.
For Ann has borne the one
who is to give birth to the Word
in a manner beyond all telling.
Overflowing with happiness,
   Ann cried out:
"Rejoice for me, all tribes of Israel,
for I will give birth
according to the will of God, my
   Benefactor.
It is he who answered my prayer
   and wiped out my shame.

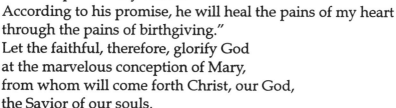

According to his promise, he will heal the pains of my heart
through the pains of birthgiving."
Let the faithful, therefore, glorify God
at the marvelous conception of Mary,
from whom will come forth Christ, our God,
the Savior of our souls.

Byzantine Liturgy

Responsory

Verse: Glorious things are said of you,
Holy Mother of God.

Response: You are the city of God,
firmly established in his holy mountain.

The Lord's Prayer

Blessing   Blessed are you, God all holy,
as part of your plan of salvation,
you prepared the Virgin Mary
to be the worthy mother of Jesus,
by sanctifying her from the time of conception.

With the help of her prayers may we be encouraged
to lead lives of constant faith and fidelity,
awaiting him who is to come: the Lord Jesus Christ.
Send your blessing upon our table,
upon those who prepared this food for us,
and make us always aware of the needs of others. Amen.

December 12: OUR LADY OF GUADALUPE

(See Common for the Feasts of the Mother of God, pages 148-149.)

December 14:
SAINT JOHN OF THE CROSS, FOUNDER AND DOCTOR

Reading   God is wise, and loves you with wisdom. God is good, and loves you
with goodness. God is holy, and loves you with holiness. God is just,
and loves you with justice. God is merciful, and loves you with mercy.
God is compassionate and understanding, and loves you with gentleness and sweetness (St. John of the Cross).

Responsory

Verse: What no eye has seen and no ear has heard,
what the mind of man cannot visualize;

Response: all that God has prepared
for those who love him (1 Cor 2:9).

The Lord's Prayer

Blessing   God of compassion and goodness,
you inspired your servant John
with a deep understanding for the mystery of the cross
and an ardent love for Jesus crucified.
By following in his footsteps,
may we carry our daily cross without complaint,
and thus come one day to the light of your glory.
Bless the food and drink at this table,
and keep us always safe under your loving protection.
We ask this through Christ our Lord.
Amen.

December 26: SAINT STEPHEN, MARTYR

Reading   The love that brought Christ from heaven to earth raised Stephen from earth to heaven. ... Love was Stephen's weapon by which he gained every battle, and so won the crown signified by his name. His love of God kept him from yielding to the ferocious mob; his love for his neighbor made him pray for those who were stoning him. Love inspired him to reprove those who erred, to make them amend, to save them from punishment. Strengthened by the power of his love, he overcame the raging cruelty of Saul and won his persecutor on earth as his companion in heaven. In his holy and tireless love he longed to gain by prayer those whom he could not convert by admonition (St. Fulgentius).

Responsory

Verse: As Stephen was being stoned he could be heard praying:

Response: "Lord Jesus, receive my spirit."

The Lord's Prayer

Blessing   Lord Jesus Christ,
           you called Saint Stephen to discipleship,
           to be the first martyr and witness
           of the early Christian church.
           Inspired by the example of his life
           may we be moved to imitate his charity and goodness
           and to love our enemies for your sake.
           Bless the food spread upon this table,
           that we may be strengthened by it for your service.
           Amen.

December 27: SAINT JOHN, APOSTLE AND EVANGELIST

Reading   My dear friends,
           if God loved us so much,
           we too should love one another.
           No one has ever seen God,
           but as long as we love one another
           God remains in us
           and his love comes to its perfection in us.

                                    1 John 4:11-12

Responsory

Verse: This is the revelation of God's love for us,

Response: that God sent his only Son into the world
          (1 Jn 4:9).

The Lord's Prayer

Blessing   Lord our God,
           your Holy Spirit filled the apostle John
           with extraordinary light concerning your mysteries,
           and with unsurpassable love for your only-begotten Son.
           Open our hearts to the good news he taught,
           and grant that we too may grow daily
           in the love of our Lord Jesus Christ.
           Bless the food and drink of your servants,
           for you alone are holy always, now and forever and ever.
           Amen.

HOLIDAYS AND SPECIAL OBSERVANCES

January 15: MARTIN LUTHER KING DAY

(Observed on the third Monday in January in commemoration of Martin Luther King's birthday.)

Reading   Let us not despair. Let us not lose faith in people and certainly not in God. We must believe that a prejudiced mind can be changed, and that people, by the grace of God, can be lifted from the valley of hate to the high mountain of love (Martin Luther King).

Responsory

Verse: Blessed are they who work for peace and justice,

Response: for they will be called children of God.

The Lord's Prayer

Blessing   Almighty God, by the hand of Moses your servant,
           you led your people out of slavery,
           and granted them freedom at the end.
           Grant that today we Christians,
           following the example of Martin Luther King,
           may resist oppression and injustice in your name,
           and may secure for all your children the liberty
           and blessed peace of the gospel of Jesus.
           Bless the food and drink at this table,
           and teach us to alleviate the hunger
           and suffering of our brothers and sisters around the world.
           We ask this in Jesus' name.
           Amen.

July 4: INDEPENDENCE DAY

Reading   Thus says Lord Yahweh:
          Look, I am beckoning to the nations
          and hoisting a signal to the peoples:
          they will bring your sons in their arms
          and your daughters will be carried on their shoulders.
          And you will know that I am Yahweh;
          those who hope in me will not be disappointed.
                                         Isaiah 49:22, 23

Responsory

Verse: For the Lord will not forsake his people;
           he will not abandon his heritage;

Response: for justice will return to the righteous,
           and all the upright in heart will follow it
           (Ps 94:14-15).

The Lord's Prayer

Blessing   Lord God almighty,
           in whose name the founders of this country
           won liberty for themselves and for us,
           and lit the torch of freedom for nations then unborn:
           Grant that we and all the people of this land
           may have grace to maintain our liberties
           in righteousness and peace;
           through Jesus Christ our Lord,
           who lives and reigns with you
           and the Holy Spirit, one God, forever and ever. Amen.
                                               Anglican Liturgy

THANKSGIVING DAY

Reading   From your lofty abode you water the mountains;
           the earth is satisfied with the fruit of your work.
           You cause the grass to grow for the cattle,
           and plants for people to use,
           to bring forth food from the earth,
           and wine to gladden the human heart,
           oil to make the face shine,
           and bread to strengthen the human heart.
                                               Psalm 104:13-15

Responsory

Verse: All [your creatures] look to you
           to give them their food in due season;

Response: when you give to them, they gather it up;
           when you open your hand,
           they are filled with good things (Ps 104:27-28).

The Lord's Prayer

Blessing   Almighty and gracious Father,
           we give you thanks for the fruits of the earth in their season
           and for the labors of those who harvest them.
           Make us, we pray, faithful stewards of your great bounty,
           for the provision of our necessities

and the relief of all who are in need,
to the glory of your name;
through Jesus Christ our Lord,
who lives and reigns with you and the Holy Spirit,
one God, now and forever. Amen.

Anglican Liturgy

November 29: DOROTHY DAY

Reading   Our Lord performed cures through contact with his sacred humanity. It is characteristic of the Son of Man to will that cure should come from contact with his sacred flesh. During his life it was the exception when he healed at a distance. "He, laying his hands on them, healed them." There was not a word about whether or not they deserved to be healed. They came to him. That was enough. He healed them (Dorothy Day).

Responsory

Verse: Suffering drives us to prayer
and we are comforted.

Response: And we are strengthened to continue our journey
in faith, and hope, and love (Dorothy Day).

The Lord's Prayer

Blessing   God of love and all consolation,
you inspired your servant Dorothy Day
to serve the poor, the hungry, and the dispossessed
all the days of her earthly life.
Look down with pity on the sufferings of the poor,
whose work and lives are hard and unrewarding,
and support all those who strive,
in the true spirit of the gospel,
for greater sharing and solidarity.
Bless the food at this table,
and grant that we may share it thankfully
with those who have less food to eat.
We ask this through Christ our Lord.
Amen.

COMMONS

For the Feasts of THE MOTHER OF GOD

Reading   Rejoice, O Mother of God,
Rejoice, O Mother of the Lamb and Shepherd!
Rejoice, O pasture of spiritual sheep!
Rejoice, O defender against unseen enemies!
Rejoice, O opening of heavenly gates!
Rejoice, for, because of you, heaven rejoices with earth,
Rejoice, O unending boast of the apostles!
Rejoice, O invincible boldness and strength of the martyrs.
Rejoice, O sure confirmation of our faith!
Rejoice, O bright knowledge and vehicle of grace!
Rejoice, for you spoiled hell forever!
Rejoice, for the Lord clothed you with his glory!
Rejoice, O Mary, the unwedded bride!

                                                 Akathist Hymn

Responsory

Verse: Rejoice, O Mary, for you gave birth to the Word,
Son of the eternal Father
and the author of all life.

Response: Accept today the homage of our prayer.
Deliver us from every calamity,
and keep us free from evil.

The Lord's Prayer

Blessing I God, our Father,
You chose the lowly maiden of Nazareth,
to become the mother of your eternal Son.
Through the intercession of her prayers
make us, your children,
grow daily in the love of you, our Father,
and in the love of all
our brothers and sisters in Christ.
Send your blessing upon our table,
upon those who prepared this food for us,
and make us always mindful

of the needs of the poor and the hungry.
We ask this of you through Jesus Christ,
Son of God and Son of Mary.
Amen.

or

Blessing II We praise and magnify you,
O Lord, the most high,
for in the fullness of time
you chose the humble virgin of Nazareth
as the mother of your only begotten Son.
By the intersession of her prayers
we beg your blessing upon our daily food and drink.
May they sustain us in our journey
until you bring us to the eternal joy of heaven,
where Jesus is king forever and ever.
Amen.

For the Feasts of PROPHETS

Reading   The task of prophecy has been to discern the signs of the times, to see what God is bringing to pass as the history of peoples and societies unfolds, to point to the judgment he brings upon all institutions (John B. Coburn).

Responsory

Verse: The prophets proclaimed what God has done
                  for us,

Response: for they grasped the meaning of his deeds.

The Lord's Prayer

Blessing   Almighty Lord, God of our ancestors,
                  you sent your prophet _____ to proclaim
                      your word
                  and to announce to the world
                  the forthcoming visitation of the redeemer.
                  Grant us, through his/her intercession,
                  the grace to serve you faithfully,
                  in peace and joy, all the days of our lives.

May your blessing descend upon our table,
so that receiving new strength,
we may continue to praise your name
forever and ever.
Amen.

For the Feasts of APOSTLES AND EVANGELISTS

Reading   So you are no longer aliens or foreign visitors;
you are fellow citizens with the holy people of
God and part of God's household. You are built
upon the foundations of the apostles and
prophets, and Christ Jesus himself is the
cornerstone. Every structure knit together in
him grows into a holy temple in the Lord; and
you too, in him, are being built up into a dwell-
ing place of God in the Spirit (Eph 2:19-21).

Responsory

Verse: "You did not choose me,
but I chose you," says the Lord,

Response: "to go forth and bear fruit that will last
forever."

The Lord's Prayer

Blessing   Almighty God,
You build the community of believers
on the foundation of the apostles and prophets.
Through them, your Holy Spirit instructs us daily,
revealing to us the mystery of Jesus Christ.
May the intercession of Saint _____
obtain for us the light of Christ on our journey,
the light which dispels all darkness
and guides us safely to the peace of your kingdom
where Christ is Lord forever.
Amen.

For the Feasts of MARTYRS

Reading   In so far as you share in the sufferings of Christ, be glad, so that you may enjoy a much greater gladness when his glory is revealed. If you are insulted for bearing Christ's name, blessed are you, for *on* you *rests the Spirit of God*, the Spirit of glory (1 Pt 4:13-14).

Responsory

Verse: The holy martyrs witnessed to Christ
           with their life and death,

Response: and with their blood
           they enriched the earth with blessings
           (Roman Office).

Blessing   We praise your name, Lord our God,
           celebrating the memory of your holy Martyr(s)_____
           whose feast we keep today.
           For the love of Christ,
           he/she (they) fought and renounced the forces of evil,
           giving us an abiding example
           of the cost of discipleship in our Christian lives.
           As we gather here to partake of this meal,
           provided for us by your loving hands,
           we thank you for the example and intersession of Saint(s) _____ ;
           may he/she (they) help us in our resolve
           to follow you with all our hearts and all our strength.
           We ask this through Christ our Lord.
           Amen.

For the Feasts of PASTORS AND CONFESSORS
(Pope, Bishop, Priest, Doctor, Abbot)

Reading   I urge the elders among you, as a fellow elder myself and a witness to the sufferings of Christ, and as one who is to have a share in the glory that is to be revealed: give a shepherd's care to the flock of God that is entrusted to you: watch over it, not simply as a duty but gladly, as God wants; not for sordid money, but because you are eager to do it. Do not lord it over the group which is in your charge, but be an example for the flock. When the chief shepherd appears, you will be given the unfading crown of glory (1 Pt 5:1-4).

Responsory

Verse: Happy are those
[whose] delight is in the law of the Lord.

Response: They are like trees planted by streams of water, which yield their fruit in its season (Ps 1:1-3).

The Lord's Prayer

Blessing   May your name be praised, Lord, our God,
for by the example and teaching of Saint _____
you have preserved your flock from the darkness of error
and have led us, your children,
into the wonderful light of Jesus Christ.
May the intersession of Saint _____
continue to guide us in truth and love,
along the path of justice and holiness of life.
Send your blessing upon our food,
and grant that we also be nourished
with the food that produces fruit for eternal life.
We ask you this in Jesus' name.
Amen.

For the Feasts of HOLY MEN

Reading   But the upright live forever,
                their recompense is with the Lord,
                and the Most High takes care of
                    them.
                So they will receive the glorious
                    crown
                and the diadem of beauty from the
                    Lord's hand;
                for he will shelter them with his
                    right hand
                and with his arm he will shield
                    them.
                                    Wisdom 5:15-16

Responsory

Verse: Put on the new self
                created in the image of God,

Response: in justice and true holiness.

The Lord's Prayer

Blessing   Lord God, our Father in heaven,
                we praise your name with joy as we recall today
                the holiness of life of Saint _____.
                May his fidelity and example continue to inspire us
                in our daily Christian lives.
                We thank you for the food on this table,
                and we pray that we may always come
                to the help of the hungry and the poor.
                We ask this in Jesus' name.
                Amen.

For the Feasts of HOLY WOMEN

Reading   On my bed at night I sought
the man who is my sweetheart:
I sought but could not find him!
So I shall get up and go through the city;
in the streets and in the squares,
I shall seek my sweetheart.
I sought but could not find him!
I came upon the watchmen—
those who go on their rounds in the city:
"Have you seen my sweetheart?"
Barely had I passed them
when I found my sweetheart.
I caught him and would not let him go.

Song of Songs 3:1-4

Responsory

Verse: Her mouth uttered words of wisdom;

Response: her tongue spoke words of compassion.

The Lord's Prayer

Blessing   Lord our God,
                 You call all your children
                 to the wedding feast
                 of your only Son, the Lord Jesus.
                 Grant us, through the intercession of Saint _____
                 to serve you faithfully
                 all the days of our earthly life,
                 and thus come one day to share
                 in the joy and blessedness
                 of the eternal banquet in you kingdom.
                 We ask this through Christ our Lord.
                 Amen.

BLESSINGS OF SPECIAL FOODS

A PRAYER FOR THE BLESSING OF HERBS

Almighty and everlasting God, by your word alone, you have made heaven and earth, and all things visible and invisible. You have enriched the earth with plants and trees for the use of people and animals. You appointed each species to bring forth fruit of its own kind, not only to serve as food for living creatures, but also as medicine for sick bodies.

With mind and body, we earnestly implore you in your goodness, to bless these various herbs and add to their natural powers the healing power of your grace. May they keep off disease and adversity from the people and animals who use them in your name. We ask you this through our Lord Jesus Christ and the intercession of his holy mother and all the saints. Amen (an old Russian prayer).

BLESSING OF CHEESE AND EGGS

O Lord our God, the creator and maker of all things, bless this curdled milk and these eggs; preserve them in your loving kindness for our use and nourishment as we partake of them. May we also be filled with your gifts, which you lavishly bestow with unspeakable goodness. For yours is the kingdom, and the power, and the glory of the Father, and of the Son, and of the Holy Spirit, now and forever and ever. Amen (a prayer from the Eastern church).

BLESSING OF GRAPES

Bless, O Lord, this new fruit of the vine, which you were pleased to bring to maturity through the passing of the seasons, the drops of the rain, and propitious weather. Let this offspring of the vine be a source of joy for those who partake of it, and may we offer it to you for the cleansing of our sins. Through the sacred body and the holy blood of Christ your Son, with whom you are blessed, together with the life-giving Spirit, now and ever and forever. Amen (a prayer from the Eastern church).

BLESSING OF BREAD

O Lord, Jesus Christ our God, you are the bread of angels and the bread that gives eternal life. You came down from heaven for our sake and fed us with the spiritual food of your divine gifts. Look upon this bread, we humbly entreat you, and as you once blessed the five loaves in the wilderness, so now also bless this bread and those who partake of it. May this blessed bread be the source of bodily and spiritual health for all those who eat it, through the grace of your love for humankind. May it be for our sanctification and the nourishment of our bodies and souls. For you are all holy, and to you we give glory, together with the Father and the Holy Spirit, now and forever and ever. Amen.

BLESSING OF DRINKING WATER

Most merciful Lord, Jesus Christ, you once sanctified the waters by accepting to be baptized in the Jordan. Grant we beseech you, to bless and sanctify this water by sending upon it the cleansing power of your Holy Spirit. May this water be a fountain of healing for the souls and bodies of all those who drink of it and entreat God's protection upon themselves. Amen (prayer from Our Lady of the Resurrection monastery).

BLESSING OF WINE

Lord, Jesus Christ, by the pleadings of your most holy mother, you once blessed and multiplied the wine at the wedding of Cana, and at the end of your earthly life you chose to transform it into your most precious blood. Grant, we ask you, to bless and multiply the wine of this holy monastery (or family) and sanctify all those who drink of it. For you are blessed forever and ever. Amen (a prayer from the Eastern church).

BLESSING FOR THE FRUITS OF THE EARTH

Father, creator of heaven and earth, you have beautified the sky with a crown of stars and illuminated it with the sun and the moon. You have also adorned the earth with its fruits to be of service and use to humankind. You have willed that all your people should rejoice in the bright shining of the sun and moon and be nourished by the fruits of the soil. Grant, we beseech you, to send us rains in abundance and to bless the earth with rich harvest and great fertility. We ask this of your goodness through your only-begotten Son, Jesus Christ our Lord. Amen (from the Apostolic Constitutions of the early church).

BLESSING OF OIL

O God, sanctify this oil which you give for the health of those who use it. As you have anointed priests, prophets, and kings, grant that this oil may likewise bestow strength and health on those who use it, through Christ our Lord. Amen (from the Apostolic Constitutions).

BLESSING OF OLIVES

O Lord, grant that the fruit of these olives may never lose their sweetness, for they are a symbol of the abundance that flows from the tree of the cross for all who put their trust in you. As you sanctify these olives, so make us strong in charity. Amen (from the Apostolic Constitutions).

BLESSING OF NEW FRUIT

O God, who by your word have bid the earth to bring forth all kinds of fruits to refresh and feed humankind and all the beasts, we thank you for these first fruits which you have given us to enjoy. We praise you for all these gifts and for all the benefits which you bestow on us through your Son, Jesus Christ our Lord. Amen (from the Apostolic Constitutions).

*P*RAYERS OF THANKSGIVING AFTER THE MEALS

We thank you, O Christ our God,
for you have filled us
with the good things of this earth.
Deprive us not of the banquet
in your heavenly kingdom,
and as once you were present among your disciples,
O Savior, and gave them peace,
come also among us and save us.
Amen.

Byzantine Prayer

V: Let us bless the Lord.

R: Thanks be to God.

✛ ✛ ✛ ✛ ✛

We thank you, Father,
for the gifts of food and fellowship at this table,
through Christ our Lord.
Amen.

V: Let us bless the Lord.

R: Thanks be to God.

✛ ✛ ✛ ✛ ✛

The blessing of God
rest upon all those who have been kind to us,
have cared for us, have worked for us, have served us,
and have shared our bread with us at this table.
Merciful God,
reward all of them according to your promise.
For yours is the kingdom, and the power, and the glory forever.
Amen.

St. Cyril of Alexandria

V: Let us bless the Lord.

R: Thanks be to God.

✛ ✛ ✛ ✛ ✛

Glory to you, O Lord, glory to you!
We give you thanks for the food
which you have given us in joy.
Fill us also with your Holy Spirit
and make us mindful of those who have less than we do.
Amen.

V: Let us bless the Lord.

R: Thanks be to God.

✝ ✝ ✝ ✝ ✝

Blessed be the Lord,
the God of our fathers and mothers,
who is merciful to us,
and nourishes us from his abundant goodness.
Glory be to the Father, to the Son,
and to the Holy Spirit, now and forever.
Amen.

V: Let us bless the Lord.

R: Thanks be to God.

✝ ✝ ✝ ✝ ✝

In peace let us pray to the Lord.
Let each of us be mindful
of all that we have received from his hands
and for which we give thanks:
food, family, friends,
work, health, and happy memories.
(Pause for silent prayer.)
So, in giving thanks we are blessed.
Amen.

Traditional Christian Prayer

V: Let us bless the Lord.

R: Thanks be to God.

✝ ✝ ✝ ✝ ✝

Alleluia!
O give thanks to the Lord, for he is good,
for his steadfast love endures forever.
[He] gives food to all flesh,
for his steadfast love endures forever.
O give thanks to the God of heaven,
for his steadfast love endures forever.
Amen.

Psalm 136:1, 25-26

V: Let us bless the Lord.

R: Thanks be to God.

Bless the Lord, O my soul,
and all that is within me,
bless his holy name.
Bless the Lord, O my soul,
and do not forget all his benefits.
Amen.

Psalm 103:1-2

V: Let us bless the Lord.

R: Thanks be to God.

Alleluia!
Praise, O servants of the Lord;
praise the name of the Lord.
Blessed be the name of the Lord
from this time on and forevermore.
From the rising of the sun to its setting
the name of the Lord is to be praised.
Amen.

Psalm 113:1-3

V: Let us bless the Lord.

R: Thanks be to God.

TABLE BLESSINGS

Alleluia!
Praise the Lord, all you nations!
Extol him, all you peoples!
For great is his steadfast love toward us,
and the faithfulness of the Lord endures forever.
Amen.

Psalm 117

V: Let us bless the Lord.

R: Thanks be to God.

✛ ✛ ✛ ✛ ✛

For this good food
and joy renewed
we praise your name, O Lord.
Amen.

A French Thanksgiving

V: Let us bless the Lord.

R: Thanks be to God.

✛ ✛ ✛ ✛ ✛

Praise God, from whom all blessings flow.
Praise him, all creatures here below,
praise him above, ye heavenly host,
praise Father, Son, and Holy Ghost.
Amen.

V: Let us bless the Lord.

R: Thanks be to God.

✛ ✛ ✛ ✛ ✛

You have filled us, O Lord, with your gifts.
As we thank you for your abundant goodness,
we ask you that this meal,
which was necessary for the strengthening of our bodies,
be also for the benefit and strengthening of our souls.
Amen.

Roman Ritual

V: Let us bless the Lord.

R: Thanks be to God.

✛ ✛ ✛ ✛ ✛

O God, our Father,
we come to you at the close of this meal in thanksgiving,
for you are the provider of our souls and bodies.
Shine in the darkness of our night
and forgive our sins and failings.
Through Christ our Lord.
Amen.

V: Let us bless the Lord.

R: Thanks be to God.

✛ ✛ ✛ ✛ ✛

May the blessing of God rest upon us,
may his peace abide with us,
may his presence illuminate our hearts
now and forevermore.
Amen.

Sufi Blessing

V: Let us bless the Lord.

R: Thanks be to God.

TABLE BLESSINGS

We thank you for your gifts, merciful God,
and we ask you to give all people the food they need.
May we all be united one day
in the eternal singing of your praises,
through Christ, our Lord.
Amen.

V: Let us bless the Lord.

R: Thanks be to God.

✤ ✤ ✤ ✤ ✤

To all else you have given us, O Lord,
we ask for but one thing more:
give us grateful hearts.
Amen.

George Herbert

V: Let us bless the Lord.

R: Thanks be to God.

✤ ✤ ✤ ✤ ✤

We thank you, almighty God,
for the food which we have received from your hands
and for the gift of fellowship at this table.
Renewed by this nourishment of body and spirit,
grant that we may continue our earthly pilgrimage
in joy and peace until we arrive one day
at the banquet feast of heaven.
Amen.

V: Let us bless the Lord.

R: Thanks be to God.

✤ ✤ ✤ ✤ ✤

May the abundance of this table never fail
and never be less, thanks to the blessing of God,
who has fed us and satisfied our needs.
To him be all glory and honor for ever.
Amen.

Armenian Prayer

V: Let us bless the Lord.

R: Thanks be to God.

✛ ✛ ✛ ✛ ✛

Compassionate and all-merciful God,
you have fed us today from the abundance of your bounty.
Fill us also with your mercy
that we may walk in joy and thanksgiving
all the days of our lives, through Christ our Lord.
Amen.

V: Let us bless the Lord.

R: Thanks be to God.

✛ ✛ ✛ ✛ ✛

God is blessed in all his gifts
and holy in all his works.
May the name of the Lord be blessed
both now and forever.
Amen.

V: Let us bless the Lord.

R: Thanks be to God.

✛ ✛ ✛ ✛ ✛

Father in heaven,
you are great in compassion
and your tenderness for us is without measure.
We thank you this day for our daily bread,
and we ask you to provide for the needs
of all your hungry children around the world.
We ask you this through Christ our Lord.
Amen.

V: Let us bless the Lord.

R: Thanks be to God.

✛ ✛ ✛ ✛ ✛

Dear Lord, we thank you
for all the material and spiritual blessings
that you have showered on us.
Help us to share all that we have
with those who are less fortunate.
We ask this in Jesus' name.
Amen.

Kent F. Warner

V: Let us bless the Lord.

R: Thanks be to God.

✛ ✛ ✛ ✛ ✛

Thank you for the world so sweet,
thank you for the food we eat,
thank you for the birds that sing,
thank you, God, for everything.
Amen.

E. Rutter Leatham

V: Let us bless the Lord.

R: Thanks be to God.

✛ ✛ ✛ ✛ ✛

Thank you, God for the food received.
Keep us ever humble, Lord,
that we may be ready recipients of your goodness.
Deliver us from pride and wickedness
and supply the wants and needs of others.
Amen.

V: Let us bless the Lord.

R: Thanks be to God.

✛ ✛ ✛ ✛ ✛

ADVENT

We give you thanks, O Lord,
for you have fed us and strengthened us
from the bounty of your providence.
The eyes of all creatures look to you
with hope awaiting your glorious coming.
Come, Lord Jesus, come!
Amen.

V: Let us bless the Lord.

R: Thanks be to God.

✛ ✛ ✛ ✛ ✛

We give you thanks, O Lord,
for you have given us food in due season.
O Emmanuel, desire of nations and Savior of all people,
come and set us free, Lord our God.
Amen.

V: Let us bless the Lord.

R: Thanks be to God.

✛ ✛ ✛ ✛ ✛

CHRISTMAS SEASON

We give you thanks, Lord Jesus
for the peace and joy of this season
and for the food we have shared in your name,
with Mary and Joseph,
with the angels and the shepherds,
with the animals and the stars.
We thank you, for the gift of your birth,
and sing to you, saying:
Glory to God in the highest,
and peace to God's people on earth.
Amen.

V: Let us bless the Lord.

R: Thanks be to God.

LENT

We give you thanks, gracious God,
for you have generously provided this food
as refreshment for our tired bodies.
Help us to remember, however,
that not on bread alone are we to live,
but on every word that comes
from the mouth of God.
Amen.

V: Let us bless the Lord.

R: Thanks be to God.

✛ ✛ ✛ ✛ ✛

We thank you, merciful God,
for the food you have given us to eat,
and for the nourishment provided to all those who are hungry.
May our lenten fasting turn us
toward all our brothers and sisters who are in need.
Amen.

V: Let us bless the Lord.

R: Thanks be to God.

✛ ✛ ✛ ✛ ✛

HOLY WEEK

Father,
for our sake Christ became obedient,
accepting even death, death on the cross.
We remember gratefully the mystery of immense love,
which he accomplished on our behalf,
and we give you thanks
for the nourishment we have received
from the abundance of your bounty.
Amen.

V: Let us bless the Lord.

R: Thanks be to God.

✠ ✠ ✠ ✠ ✠

EASTER SEASON

Lord God, source of all life,
we give you thanks for the resurrection of Jesus
and for the gift of renewed life in him.
We are grateful for the food received at this table.
May we always recognize Christ's presence
in the breaking of the bread.
Amen.

V: Let us bless the Lord.

R: Thanks be to God.

✠ ✠ ✠ ✠ ✠

We joyfully give you thanks, O Lord,
for having partaken of this meal
in the gladness of the resurrection.
Remain always present with us,
until the day you call us
to the banquet feast of heaven.
Amen.

V: Let us bless the Lord.

R: Thanks be to God.

✠ ✠ ✠ ✠ ✠

ASCENSION

Lord Jesus Christ,
you gloriously ascended into heaven
and promised to your disciples to send upon them
the Comforter, the Spirit of Truth and Love.

May the Holy Spirit abide always with us,
as we daily pray in thanksgiving for all the gifts received
from your goodness without measure.
Amen.

V: Let us bless the Lord.

R: Thanks be to God.

✛ ✛ ✛ ✛ ✛

PENTECOST

Lord God,
you have renewed the earth by the power of the Holy Spirit.
May the Holy Spirit remain always with us
as we daily give you thanks,
for all the gifts received from your goodness and mercy.
Amen.

V: Let us bless the Lord.

R: Thanks be to God.

✛ ✛ ✛ ✛ ✛

FEASTS OF THE LORD

Lord God,
You are present in all living things
and nourish them with your goodness.
We give you thanks for our Lord Jesus Christ,
for the food and fellowship at this table,
which give us new strength to persevere in your service.
Amen.

V: Let us bless the Lord.

R: Thanks be to God.

✛ ✛ ✛ ✛ ✛

FEASTS OF OUR LADY

O Lord, our God, with Mary we proclaim
  your wonders
and rejoice in Christ, our Savior.
Through him, you have filled us with good
  things,
giving us our daily bread
and the strength needed for your service.
We give you thanks and glory, therefore,
  O Lord,
and by the prayers of the Mother of God,
we ask you to render good
to all those who have helped us for the sake
  of your name.
Amen.

V: Let us bless the Lord.

R: Thanks be to God.